**BARRON'S** Let's Prepare for the

# PARCC

## GRADE 4 ELA/LITERACY TEST

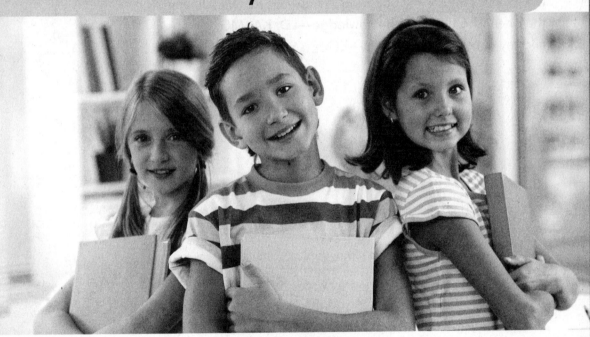

Kelli Eppley, M.S.
Principal
Robinson Elementary School
Trenton, New Jersey

## About the Author

Kelli Eppley, M.S., is the Principal of Robinson Elementary School. Prior to that, she was the Supervisor of English Language Arts in the Hamilton Township School District for seven years, and an elementary school teacher for six years. Her area of expertise is in elementary reading and writing. She also teaches a teacher preparation class at the college level. Kelli obtained her master's degree from Rutgers University in Educational Leadership. She also has additional graduate work in reading and writing instruction. She has been training teachers on the Common Core Standards and the PARCC assessment for the past three years.

## Acknowledgments

Many thanks to:

the loves of my life for believing in me—JE, RE, ML, JL, and IK;

the ones who fill me with knowledge—LD, KA, MG;

and my constant cheerleader—EG.

All inquiries should be addressed to:
Barron's Educational Series, Inc.
250 Wireless Boulevard
Hauppauge, NY 11788
www.barronseduc.com

ISBN: 978-1-4380-0813-4

Library of Congress Control Number 2016937245

Manufactured by: B11R11
Date of Manufacture: June 2016

Printed in the United States of America

9 8 7 6 5 4 3 2 1

10% POST-CONSUMER WASTE
Paper contains a minimum of 10% post-consumer waste (PCW). Paper used in this book was derived from certified, sustainable forestlands.

# Contents

# Chapter 4
# Research Simulation Task       **63**

# Chapter 5
# Narrative Writing Task       **93**

# Chapter 6
# Test-Taking Strategies
# for Computer-Based Testing       **121**

# Overview of PARCC Grade 4

## Introduction for Students

Fourth-grade students in many states across the country will be taking an important test in the spring. This test is called the PARCC Assessment (Partnership for Assessment of Readiness for College and Careers). The PARCC Assessment has two different tests that cover Mathematics and English Language Arts.

The PARCC Assessment is given after 75 percent of the school year is completed. The test focuses on reading comprehension, writing, and text analysis. In case you were a third grader during the 2014–2015 school year, please note that the testing format of the PARCC was recently revised to reduce the amount of testing time. The test was previously administered at two different times during the school year. In 2016 and beyond, the test will only be given once during the school year.

You will be taking this test on a computer. That is enough to make your knees shake—YIKES! Believe it or not, you really do not need to be nervous. You and your teachers have been preparing for this since Kindergarten!

Just in case those words of assurance do not completely convince you, this book is designed to prove to you that YOU ARE READY. The helpful hints and sample tests included in this book have been tested in a classroom with other fourth-grade students just like you, and will give you the confidence you need to do your very best work on the English Language Arts section of the tests.

Here is some information about the test that will help you understand what you will be asked to do.

The English Language Arts portion of the PARCC assessment is comprised of three units. Each unit is 90 minutes long. When taking the test, you will need to do the following:

- Read literature and informational texts
- Write a narrative story
- Write a literary analysis
- Write an informational text that integrates ideas from multiple sources (research)
- Answer two-part multiple-choice questions
- Answer technology-enhanced questions (drag and drop, highlight, etc.)

Since you will use the computer to take the test, practice your typing skills so you can easily type your responses. It will also be helpful if you time yourself while taking the tests, so you can experience what it feels like to type your responses within the time limits of the actual test. Also practice using the mouse or touch pad/touch screen to select items, drag and drop, highlight, and scroll, as these are all things you will be required to do when taking the test.

By knowing what to expect and practicing your skills in advance, you will be in the best-possible position to succeed on all components of the PARCC Assessment of English Language Arts.

In this book, you will find each of the main sections of the test explained in their own chapters. Each chapter includes additional opportunities for independent practice, and all questions have detailed explanations of the correct answers. In addition to the practice exercises accompanying each chapter, two complete practice tests are included at the end of the book. Once you have completed practicing each section, you can test yourself by taking these tests.

---

**IMPORTANT NOTE:** Barron's has made every effort to ensure the content of this book is accurate as of press time, but the PARCC Assessments are constantly changing. Be sure to consult *http://www.parcconline.org* for all the latest testing information. Regardless of the changes that may be announced after press time, this book will still provide a strong framework for fourth-grade students preparing for the assessment.

## Overview for Parents and Teachers

This book is designed to help fourth-grade students achieve proficiency on the English Language Arts portion of the PARCC Assessment. In addition to two complete practice tests, it includes instructional study units in the following four skill areas:

1. Understanding test-taking strategies

2. Reading literature and writing a narrative response

3. Reading literature and writing a literary analysis

4. Reading informational texts and writing in response to a research task

## What to Expect

Students will be introduced to strategies that will help them build familiarity with the test format while gaining confidence in the individual tasks required. Checklists and rubrics (scoring guides for student writing) are provided and explained. These will help the students understand what is expected and how their work will be scored.

Ample opportunities are available for both guided and independent practice of each portion of the test. Two complete PARCC practice tests are included, so students can get a feel of what the actual test will be like.

## Testing Times and Formats

The ELA portion of the PARCC is comprised of three units. The units may not be given in the order listed below. Schools may administer one or more units per day.

### Unit 1: Literary Analysis Task—90 minutes

- Read one extended literature text and one short literature text
- Answer six multiple-choice/technology-enhanced questions
- Complete one literary analysis task, based on the texts read
- Read one short passage (either fiction or nonfiction) and answer four multiple-choice/technology-enhanced questions

## Unit 2: Research Simulation Task—90 minutes

- Read/view one extended informational text and two short informational texts. One of these could be a video or graphic (chart, table, map, infographic, etc.).
- Answer eight multiple-choice/technology-enhanced questions
- Complete one research simulation task, based on the texts read/viewed

## Unit 3: Narrative Writing Task—90 minutes

- Read one short narrative text
- Answer four multiple-choice/technology-enhanced questions
- Complete one narrative writing task, based on the text
- Read one long passage or one paired set of texts
- Answer six multiple-choice/technology-enhanced questions

The units and testing items described above are based on the Spring 2016 administration of the PARCC Assessment. These units reflect recent changes that aimed to reduce the overall testing time of the PARCC.

## How the PARCC Is Given

The PARCC Assessment is taken on the computer using an online testing system called TestNav. You will be asked to read passages and answer different types of questions on the computer. Examples of the different types of questions are shown below and are excerpted from the Practice Test—Grade 4, which can be found at *http://www.parcconline.com*

Below is an example of an Evidence-Based Selected-Response question. This type of multiple-choice question has two parts. In Part A, you are asked to provide an answer to a question, and in Part B, you are asked to provide evidence to support your answer in Part A.

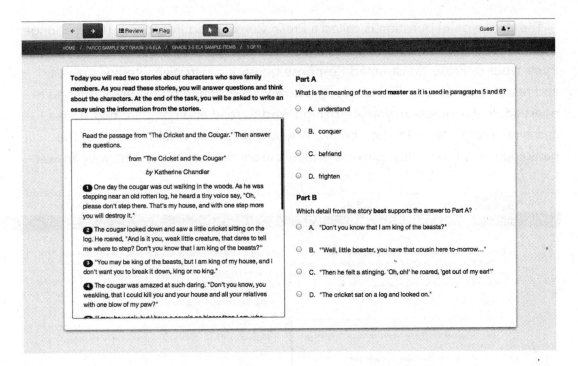

The next type of question is a Technology-Enhanced Constructed-Response question. For this type of question, you are asked to click, drag, highlight, or select your response. In this specific question, you are asked to drag and drop three details from the story into the setting box at the bottom of the screen.

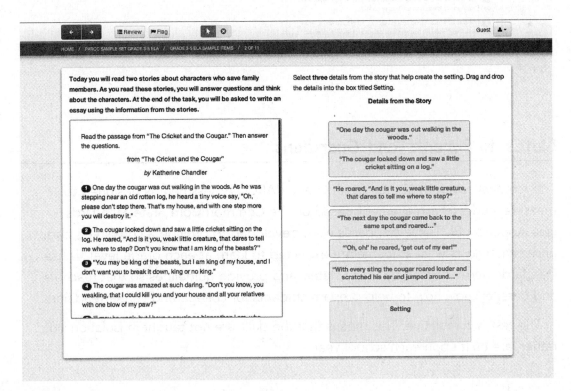

The third type of question is called a Prose Constructed Response. This is a longer piece of writing that is connected to one or more texts that you will read. There are three types of Prose Constructed-Response questions: narrative, literary analysis, and research simulation. The question below is an example of a Literary Analysis question. In this question, you are being asked to read and compare two stories and type a response in the box below. A typical response would be four or five paragraphs long. You must provide evidence from the text to support your answer.

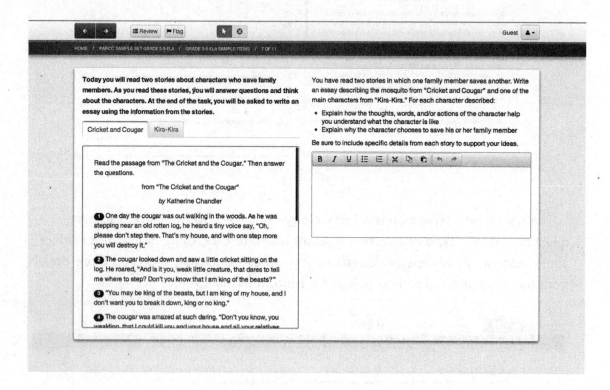

## Notes to Parents and Guardians

The material covered on the Fourth Grade PARCC Assessment is designed to measure students' achievement based on the Common Core State Standards (see Appendix B). These standards were developed to provide a consistent, clear understanding of what students are expected to learn at each grade level. These standards were adopted by many states, and provide guidelines so that teachers and parents know how to help prepare students for college and career readiness.

The test is cumulative. This means that the skills are not taught in isolation but, rather, are built upon each school year.

Some students are unnerved by the fact that the test is timed. They worry that they will run out of time before they finish. Practice tests, like the two included in this book, are a good way to put these fears to rest. As students become more familiar with the skills required, taking the test becomes less frightening.

When preparing for this test, common sense should prevail. Provide a quiet place for your child to complete homework every evening. Encourage your child to read each day to themselves and also out loud to you. It is especially helpful if you make time to read out loud to him or her too! Talk about your child's school experiences together. Try to get a sense of how he or she feels about what is being learned in fourth grade.

In addition, because the test is given on the computer, your child should practice typing skills and be able to comfortably work on whatever testing device your school district plans to use during the assessment period (e.g., PC, laptop, tablet device).

As with any standardized test experience, be sure that your child gets a good night's rest and eats a healthy breakfast before coming to school on test days. Feeling good physically can promote a positive attitude toward the test experience.

Finally, after all the preparation is done and the tests are over, the most common question is usually, "When can I expect to see the results?" School districts usually receive test scores sometime during the month of June. However, it is not uncommon for them to be distributed early the following school year.

## Score Reports

Your child's test scores will be provided in a detailed report. The first score you will see is an overall performance level. This is provided as a score between 650–850 and a performance level from 1–5. It will look similar to the graphic below.

Child's Score: 739

| 650 | 700 | 725 | 750 | 803 | 850 |
|-----|-----|-----|-----|-----|-----|
| LEVEL 1 | LEVEL 2 | LEVEL 3 | LEVEL 4 | LEVEL 5 | |

| School average | District average | State average | PARCC average |
|----------------|------------------|--------------|---------------|
| 741 | 765 | 745 | 739 |

Students who score in the level 1 and 2 range are not yet meeting the standards and are showing a need for academic improvement. Students who score at a level three are approaching the standards, and students who score at a level 4 or 5 are meeting or exceeding the standards and are on-track for college and career readiness.

The score report will also show the school, district, state, and PARCC average performance score. This will allow you to see how your child compares to other students in your school, town, state, and across the country.

The score report also provides a breakdown for a student's performance in reading and writing. In reading, students can score between 10 and 90 points. In writing, students can score between 10 and 60 points. Additionally, parents can see what a "meeting expectations" score is, as well as a school, district, and state average.

Reading and writing are both broken into subsections that show if your child is performing below expectations, nearly meeting expectations, or meeting or exceeding expectations.

---

**READING**

| Reading score range:<br>10 to 90<br>Your child's score | Average of students<br>just meeting expectations<br>50 | School average<br>52 |
|---|---|---|
| **44** | District average<br>48 | State average<br>45 |

**LITERARY TEXT**

⬇ **In this area, your child did not do as well as students who met the expectations.**

Students meet expectations by showing they can read and analyze grade appropriate fiction, drama and poetry.

**INFORMATIONAL TEXT**

⬌ **In this area, your child did almost as well as students who met the expectations.**

Students meet expectations by showing they can read and analyze grade-appropriate non-fiction, including texts about history, science, art, and music.

**VOCABULARY**

⬆ **In this area, your child did as well as or better than students who met the expectations.**

Students meet expectations by showing they can use context to determine what words and phrases mean in grade-appropriate texts.

---

**WRITING**

| Writing score range:<br>10 to 60<br>Your child's score: | Average of students<br>just meeting expectations<br>35 | School average<br>39 |
|---|---|---|
| **30** | District average<br>35 | State average<br>31 |

**WRITING EXPRESSION**

⬇ **In this area, your child did not do as well as students who met the expectations.**

Students meet expectations by showing they can compose well-developed, organized, and clear writing, using details from what they have read.

**KNOWLEDGE AND USE OF LANGUAGE CONVENTIONS**

⬆ **In this area, your child did as well as or better than students who met the expectations.**

Students meet expectations by showing they can compose writing using the rules of standard English, including those for grammar, spelling, and usage.

**LEGEND**

⬇ Below Expectations ⬌ Nearly Meets Expectations ⬆ Meets or Exceeds Expectations

To see selected questions from the test, visit understandthescore.org.

---

More detailed information about understanding the PARCC Score Reports can be found at *http://UnderstandTheScore.org*.

## What Is the Common Core?

The Common Core refers to a common and clear set of guidelines outlining what all students should know in Math and English in grades K–12. These guidelines were created to prepare students for college and/or career.

## What Are the Common Core Standards?

The standards provide guidelines for teachers and parents on what should be taught at each grade level. Teachers still have flexibility in how the content is taught. These rigorous standards will prepare students for the 21st Century. Forty-five states, as well as the District of Columbia, are using these standards.

## How Does This Impact Education?

Educators have been using standards for many years. The Common Core is the newest set of standards adopted by many states. Standards set a goal that students must meet by the end of the school year. The standards do not tell teachers how to teach, but they instruct teachers on what content must be covered in a specific grade level. The PARCC test was developed to determine how successful students are with mastering these standards.

## Information About the Standards

The standards are broken into several sections: Reading Literature, Reading Informational Text, Foundational Reading Skills, Speaking and Listening, Writing, and Language. Each section outlines some of the things that students should be able to do in each area, at each grade level. A complete list of the standards can be found in Appendix B.

## Reading: Literature

Reading Literature focuses on reading works of fiction—stories, plays, poetry, etc. In fourth grade, students are asked to read literature closely to make inferences, summarize, determine theme, and describe plot elements in depth (character, setting, etc.). Students are also expected to determine the meaning of words, compare and contrast (structure, elements of texts, and theme, etc.), make connections, and read a variety of grade-level fiction.

## Reading: Informational Text

Reading Informational Texts focuses on reading works of nonfiction— articles, technical texts, biographies, etc. In fourth grade, students are asked to read informational texts and make inferences, determine the main idea, summarize, and explain procedures or concepts. Students are also expected to determine the meaning of words, describe the structure of the text, and compare and contrast multiple texts on the same topic. In addition, students are asked to examine visual elements (charts, graphs, etc.) and explain how claims are supported with details. Finally, they should read a variety of grade-level informational texts.

## Reading: Foundational Skills

Foundational skills are the phonics and fluency skills that students need to read the words in a given text. In fourth grade, students are expected to use more advanced phonics skills to decode words. Students are also expected to read with expression and accuracy, and to self-correct when they make errors while reading.

## Speaking and Listening

The Speaking and Listening standards seek to develop discussion, collaboration, and presentation skills for students. Students are expected to actively participate in group discussions, paraphrase what a text says, and identify reasons and support given by the speaker. Students will also be expected to present their ideas and identify the conversational patterns that are appropriate in formal and informal situations.

## Writing

The Writing standards focus on the writing process and require students to write for a variety of purposes. Three types of writing are clearly outlined by the standards—narrative writing (a story), informational writing (nonfiction), and opinion-based writing (persuasive). The standards also require students to revise their own work and publish writing using a computer.

## Language

The Language standards focus on grammar, capitalization, punctuation, and language use. Students are expected to use strong vocabulary and figurative language in their writing. Spelling is also addressed in the language standards.

## Should My Child Take the PARCC Assessment?

You may have seen media coverage of the PARCC Assessment that indicates that the PARCC Assessment might be stressful or harmful to students. While standardized testing does carry high stakes, the PARCC assessment replaces state developed tests that were given previously.

Some parents worry that their children will be uncomfortable using the computer to take the test. Most students have indicated that they enjoyed using the computer to take the test and were comfortable with the online platform.

Participation in the PARCC Assessment provides valuable information for schools and parents. If you have questions about how the PARCC Assessment might impact your child, or are considering "opting out" of the assessment, please contact your child's teacher or principal to get more information so that you can make an informed decision for your child and your family.

# Answering Multiple-Choice and Technology-Enhanced Questions on the PARCC

# CHAPTER 2

## Overview

On the PARCC Assessment, you will be asked to answer multiple-choice and technology-enhanced questions about literature and informational text.

Literature is a narrative text that is written to tell a story. The literature on the PARCC Assessment is taken directly from the published work of authors. This might be from a picture book or an excerpt from a longer work like a chapter book. Informational text is nonfiction text that is factual. The informational text might be an article, a biography, or an essay. The selections that you will read can be relatively short (200 words) or longer (800 words). Sometimes there will be two separate texts about a similar topic that you will need to read.

There are many strategies for reading literature and informational text. The chart below gives examples of strategies to use before and during the reading of the passage on the test. The last two columns tell you if a strategy is effective for literature, informational text, or both.

**TIP:** *Remember to adjust the volume of the computer before the test begins.*

| Before Reading Strategies | Description | Literature | Informational Text |
|---|---|---|---|
| Directions | Be sure that you understand the directions on the test. Listen carefully to all of the directions and reread them if you are unsure of what you need to do on a section of the test. | X | X |
| Genre | Identify the genre of the text, and think about what you know about that genre. | X | X |

| Before Reading Strategies | Description | Literature | Informational Text |
|---|---|---|---|
| Title Predictions | Read the title of the text, and predict what you think the story will be about. Thinking about what you will be reading about will help you activate your background knowledge about the topic. | X | X |
| Preview the Passage | Preview the passage to determine the length and organization. Read all headings, titles, and captions. Look at the graphics and visuals in the passage. | X | X |
| Preview the Questions | Read the questions before you begin reading the passages. Reading the questions first will help you to understand what part of the text to focus on. | X | X |
| Read and Pause | Stop after each paragraph or section to think about what you are reading. Make sure that you understand what you just read. If you don't understand it, go back and reread the section. | X | X |
| Notes | Make notes on your scrap paper about what you are reading. You might want to write down comments or questions that come to mind while you are reading. | X | X |
| Question | Ask yourself questions while you are reading. Look for answers as you continue reading. | X | X |
| Make Connections | Think about how the text connects to you, the world, or other texts/videos that you have read/seen. These connections will help you understand what is happening while you are reading. | X | X |
| Visualize | Make pictures in your head while you are reading. These pictures will help you see what the author is trying to say. | X | X |

| Before Reading Strategies | Description | Literature | Informational Text |
|---|---|---|---|
| Purpose | What is the author's purpose for writing this story or informational text? The author might be writing to persuade, entertain, or inform. | X | X |
| Story Elements | Think about the characters, setting, problem, and solution in the story. All stories will have these literary elements. Often, there will be several attempts to solve a problem or problems in the story. Identifying these elements can help you summarize the story. | X | |
| Font | Pay attention to words in **bold** or *italics*. These will be important words in the story. Sometimes, these words are asked about in vocabulary questions. | | X |
| Context Clues | Use words, sentences, and pictures in the passage to give you clues about the meaning of words that you don't understand. Reading on is a strategy for using context clues where the reader continues to read the sentence to attempt to determine the meaning of a word. | X | X |

After you read one or more passages, you will be asked to answer questions. The first type of question will be multiple choice. The test developers call these questions Evidenced-Based Selected-Response questions. What is unique about these questions is that they have two parts to each question. In Part A, readers will be asked a question about the text that they read. In Part B, readers will be asked to provide evidence from the text to support their answer in Part A.

## Strategies for Answering Multiple-Choice (EBSR) Questions

- Read the question carefully.
- Predict the answer before you read the answer choices.
- Read all the answer choices. Use process of elimination to select the answer that makes the most sense. Use the answer elimination tool to cross out choices that you know are wrong.
- Answer the questions that you think are the easiest first. Skip the ones that are hard, and go back to them at the end of the session.
- Answer every question.
- Read carefully when you see words like *always* or *never*.
- Reread the text.

The second type of question is called a Technology-Enhanced Constructed-Response question. These questions are answered through the use of technology. Many of these questions will seem familiar to activities you have done in your classroom, using paper and pencil. These questions will require you to drag and drop, highlight, select, and move objects on the test. It is important to practice these tasks on the computer before the test.

## Strategies for Answering Technology-Enhanced Constructed-Response Questions

- Read the task carefully. Be sure that you understand all of the parts of the question.
- Be sure that you complete all parts of the task.
- Reread the text.
- Use technology carefully to ensure that your answer will count.

# GUIDED PRACTICE—MULTIPLE-CHOICE

Now that you understand the types of passages and questions on the test, you can practice using the strategies to answer both types of questions. Read "A Fairy Story" carefully. There are two multiple-choice questions after the story, with explanations. Be sure to read the explanations carefully.

### A Fairy Story: An Excerpt from *Rebecca of Sunnybrook Farm*
#### by Kate Douglas Wiggins

1   There was once a tired and rather poverty-stricken Princess who dwelled in a cottage on the great highway between two cities. She was not as unhappy as thousands of others; indeed, she had much to be grateful for, but the life she lived and the work she did were hard for one who was so slender.

2   Now the cottage stood by the edge of a great green forest where the wind was always singing in the branches and the sunshine filtering through the leaves.

3   And one day when the Princess was sitting by the wayside quite tired from her labor in the fields, she saw a golden chariot rolling down the King's Highway and in it a person who could be none other than somebody's Fairy Godmother on her way to the Court. The chariot halted at her door, and though the Princess had read of such generous persons, she never dreamed for an instant that one of them could ever alight at her cottage.

4   "If you are tired, poor little Princess, why do you not go into the cool green forest and rest?" asked the Fairy Godmother.

5   "Because I have no time," she answered. "I must go back to my plow."

6   "Is that your plow leaning by the tree, and is it not too heavy?"

7   "It is heavy," answered the Princess, "but I love to turn the hard earth into soft furrows and know that I am making good soil where

my seeds may grow. When I feel the weight too much, I try to think of the harvest."

8    The golden chariot passed on, and the two talked no more together that day; nevertheless the King's messengers were busy, for they whispered one word into the ear of the Fairy Godmother and another into the ear of the Princess, though so faintly that neither of them realized that the King had spoken.

9    The next morning a strong man knocked at the cottage door, and doffing his hat to the Princess said: "A golden chariot passed me yesterday, and one within it flung me a purse of coins, saying: Go out into the King's Highway and search until you find a cottage and a heavy plow leaning against a tree nearby. Enter and say to the Princess whom you will find there: "I will guide the plow and you must go and rest, or walk in the cool green forest; for this is the command of your Fairy Godmother."

10    And the same thing happened every day, and every day the tired Princess walked in the green wood. Many times she caught the glitter of the chariot and ran into the Highway to give thanks to the Fairy Godmother; but she was never fleet enough to reach the spot. She could only stand with eager eyes and longing heart as the chariot passed by. Yet she never failed to catch a smile, and sometimes a word or two floated back to her, words that sounded like: "I would not be thanked. We are all children of the same King, and I am only his messenger."

**11** Now as the Princess walked daily in the green forest, hearing the wind singing in the branches and seeing the sunlight filter through the lattice-work of green leaves, there came into her thoughts that had lain asleep in the stifling air of the cottage and the weariness of guiding the plow. And by and by she took a needle from her girdle and pricked the thoughts on the leaves of the trees and sent them into the air to float hither and thither. And it came to pass that people began to pick them up, and holding them against the sun, to read what was written on them, and this was because the simple little words on the leaves were only, after all, a part of one of the King's messages, such as the Fairy Godmother dropped continually from her golden chariot.

**12** But the miracle of the story lies deeper than all this.

**13** Whenever the Princess pricked the words upon the leaves she added a thought of her Fairy Godmother, and folding it close within, sent the leaf out on the breeze to float hither and thither and fall where it would. And many other little Princesses felt the same impulse and did the same thing. And as nothing is ever lost in the King's Dominion, so these thoughts and wishes and hopes, being full of love and gratitude, had no power to die, but took unto themselves other shapes and lived on forever. They cannot be seen, our vision is too weak; nor heard, our hearing is too dull; but they can sometimes be felt, and we know not what force is stirring our hearts to nobler aims.

**14** The end of the story is not come, but it may be that some day when the Fairy Godmother has a message to deliver in person straight to the King, he will say: "Your face I know; your voice, your thoughts, and your heart. I have heard the rumble of your chariot wheels on the great Highway, and I knew that you were on the King's business. Here in my hand is a sheaf of messages from every quarter of my kingdom. They were delivered by weary and footsore travelers, who said that they could never have reached the gate in safety had it not been for your help and inspiration. Read them, that you may know when and where and how you sped the King's service."

15 And when the Fairy Godmother reads them, it may be that sweet odors will rise from the pages, and half-forgotten memories will stir the air; but in the gladness of the moment nothing will be half so lovely as the voice of the King when he said: "Read, and know how you sped the King's service."

1. **Part A**

What is the meaning of the word **labor** as it is used in paragraph 3 of "A Fairy Story"?

○ A. follow rules
○ B. rest
○ C. work
○ D. plant crops

**Part B**

Which detail from the story **best** helps the reader understand the meaning of **labor**?

○ A. "The chariot halted at her door, and though the Princess had read of such generous persons, she never dreamed for an instant that one of them could ever alight at her cottage." (paragraph 3)
○ B. "'It is heavy,' answered the Princess, 'but I love to turn the hard earth into soft furrows and know that I am making good soil where my seeds may grow.'" (paragraph 7)
○ C. "And by and by she took a needle from her girdle and pricked the thoughts on the leaves of the trees and sent them into the air to float hither and thither." (paragraph 11)
○ D. "Here in my hand is a sheaf of messages from every quarter of my kingdom." (paragraph 14)

## Answers and Explanation

In Part A, the correct answer is **(C)**—*work*. This is correct because the sentence indicates that that she was tired from her **labor** in the fields. Follow rules and rest would not make sense in this sentence. Plant crops might seem like the correct answer, but work is a better choice because it includes a variety of tasks that she might do in the field, such as plowing, planting, and watering. In Part B, the correct answer is **(B)**. This answer shows how the Princess is working in the field. The other sentences talk about different parts of the story and do not show how hard the Princess was working.

2. **Part A**

   Which statement **best** expresses one of the themes in the story?

   ○  A.  Believe in the wisdom of others.
   ○  B.  The actions of one can impact the actions of many.
   ○  C.  Do not be afraid of others.
   ○  D.  We can all learn how to do new things from others.

   **Part B**

   Which sentence **best** provides evidence that supports the theme that you selected in Part A.

   ○  A.  "They cannot be seen, our vision is too weak; nor heard, our hearing is too dull; but they can sometimes be felt, and we know not what force is stirring our hearts to nobler aims." (paragraph 13)
   ○  B.  "Go out into the King's Highway and search until you find a cottage and a heavy plow leaning against a tree nearby." (paragraph 9)
   ○  C.  "'If you are tired, poor little Princess, why do you not go into the cool green forest and rest?' asked the Fairy Godmother." (paragraph 4)
   ○  D.  "There was once a tired and rather poverty-stricken Princess who dwelled in a cottage on the great highway between two cities." (paragraph 1)

## Answers and Explanation

In Part A, the correct answer is **(B)**—*The actions of one can impact the actions of many.* This is correct because in the story, the actions of the Fairy Godmother impact many people in the Kingdom in a positive way. Choice (C) does not make sense for this story, and can be eliminated. Choices (A) and (D) apply to some aspects of the story but do not encompass the entire story. In Part B, the correct answer is **(A)**. This sentence is talking about the impact that the Princess's leaves have had on the Kingdom. If the Fairy Godmother had not sent the man to the Princess's house, which allowed her to rest, the messages would not have been created. This shows how the actions of the Fairy Godmother have impacted many people.

# GUIDED PRACTICE—
# TECHNOLOGY-ENHANCED QUESTIONS

Now you will answer some technology-enhanced questions about *A Fairy Story*. Following are two technology-enhanced questions, with explanations. Be sure to read the explanations carefully. Although these questions are usually answered on the computer, you can practice understanding the content through this book. The questions on the computer will use words like drag, drop, and highlight. For the purpose of this book, you will write the answers in the boxes provided.

## Technology-Enhanced Question 1

Select two details that help establish the setting of the story. Write the details in the box labeled setting.

- "She was not as unhappy as thousands of others; indeed, she had much to be grateful for, but the life she lived and the work she did were hard for one who was so slender." (paragraph 1)
- "Now the cottage stood by the edge of a great green forest where the wind was always singing in the branches and the sunshine filtering through the leaves." (paragraph 2)
- "But the miracle of the story lies deeper than all this." (paragraph 12)
- "And by and by she took a needle from her girdle and pricked the thoughts on the leaves of the trees and sent them into the air to float hither and thither." (paragraph 11)
- "There was once a tired and rather poverty-stricken Princess who dwelled in a cottage on the great highway between two cities." (paragraph 1)
- "They were delivered by weary and footsore travelers, who said that they could never have reached the gate in safety had it not been for your help and inspiration." (paragraph 14)

**Setting**

## Answers and Explanation

The correct answer is in the box below. These two details tell about the setting of the story. The setting is the time or place that a story takes place.

**Setting**

- Now the cottage stood by the edge of a great green forest where the wind was always singing in the branches and the sunshine filtering through the leaves.
- There was once a tired and rather poverty-stricken Princess who dwelled in a cottage on the great highway between two cities.

## Technology-Enhanced Question 2

Create a summary of the story by selecting **three** key events from the list below. Write the events in the box in the order that they happened.

- The people in the Kingdom found the messages and were inspired to continue on their journey.
- The man plowed the field.
- The Fairy Godmother drove her chariot down the road.
- The Fairy Godmother saw that the Princess was tired and sent someone to help her.
- The Princess worked hard in the field.
- The Princess walked in the forest and wrote messages on leaves.

| Event 1 |
| --- |
| |

| Event 2 |
| --- |
| |

| Event 3 |
| --- |
| |

## Answers and Explanation

The correct answer is in the boxes below. The three events that were selected summarize the most important parts of the story and are placed in the correct order. The other events are less important details.

**Event 1**

The Fairy Godmother saw that the Princess was tired and sent someone to help her.

**Event 2**

The Princess walked in the forest and wrote messages on leaves.

**Event 3**

The people in the Kingdom found the messages and were inspired to continue on their journey.

## INDEPENDENT PRACTICE

Read "Your Amazing Brain" carefully. There are three multiple-choice and two technology-enhanced questions after the story. Read the questions and try to answer them to the best of your ability. Although the technology questions are usually completed on the computer, you can write your answers in the boxes provided. The answers are at the end of the chapter.

### Your Amazing Brain
by Douglas A. Richards

1    You carry around a three-pound mass of wrinkly material in your head that controls every single thing you will ever do. From enabling you to think, learn, create, and feel emotions to controlling every blink, breath, and heartbeat—this fantastic control center is your brain. It is a structure so amazing that a famous scientist once called it "the most complex thing we have yet discovered in our universe."

**Your brain is faster and more powerful than a supercomputer.**

2   Your kitten is on the kitchen counter. She's about to step onto a hot stove. You have only seconds to act. Accessing the signals coming from your eyes, your brain quickly calculates when, where, and at what speed you will need to dive to intercept her. Then it orders your muscles to do so. Your timing is perfect and she's safe. No computer can come close to your brain's awesome ability to download, process, and react to the flood of information coming from your eyes, ears, and other sensory organs.

**Your brain generates enough electricity to power a light bulb.**

3   Your brain contains about 100 billion microscopic cells called neurons—so many it would take you over 3,000 years to count them all. Whenever you dream, laugh, think, see, or move, it's because tiny chemical and electrical signals are racing between these neurons along billions of tiny neuron highways. Believe it or not, the activity in your brain never stops. Countless messages zip around inside it every second like a supercharged pinball machine. Your neurons create and send more messages than all the phones in the entire world. And while a single neuron generates only a tiny amount of electricity, all your neurons together can generate enough electricity to power a low-wattage bulb.

4   Neurons send information to your brain at more than 150 miles (241 kilometers) per hour.

5   A bee lands on your bare foot. Sensory neurons in your skin relay this information to your spinal cord and brain at a speed of more than 150 miles (241 kilometers) per hour. Your brain then uses motor neurons to transmit the message back through your spinal cord to your foot to shake the bee off quickly. Motor neurons can relay this information at more than 200 miles (322 kilometers) per hour.

### When you learn, you change the structure of your brain.

6   Riding a bike seems impossible at first. But soon you master it. How? As you practice, your brain sends "bike riding" messages along certain pathways of neurons over and over, forming new connections. In fact, the structure of your brain changes every time you learn, as well as whenever you have a new thought or memory.

### Exercise helps make you smarter.

7   It is well known that any exercise that makes your heart beat faster, like running or playing basketball, is great for your body and can even help improve your mood. But scientists have recently learned that for a period of time after you've exercised, your body produces a chemical that makes your brain more receptive to learning. So if you're stuck on a homework problem, go out and play a game of soccer, then try the problem again. You just might discover that you're able to solve it.

**1. Part A**

Why did the author write this article?

- A. To inform us how our brain controls everything we think, say, and do.
- B. To persuade us to use our brains.
- C. To entertain us with stories of how the brain works.
- D. To express that the brain is the most important organ in the body.

**Part B**

What sentence from the story **best** supports your answer in Part A.

- A. "Your kitten is on the kitchen counter." (paragraph 2)
- B. "From enabling you to think, learn, create, and feel emotions to controlling every blink, breath, and heartbeat—this fantastic control center is your brain." (paragraph 1)
- C. "So if you're stuck on a homework problem, go out and play a game of soccer, then try the problem again." (paragraph 7)
- D. "Your brain contains about 100 billion microscopic cells called neurons—so many it would take you over 3,000 years to count them all." (paragraph 3)

2. **Part A**

   In the phrase "you will need to dive to intercept her," what does **intercept** mean as it is used in paragraph 2 of "Your Amazing Brain"?

   ○ A. encourage

   ● B. stop or prevent the course of

   ○ C. gain possession of the ball

   ○ D. sustain

   **Part B**

   Which of the sentences from the passage **best** helps the reader understand the meaning of **intercept**?

   ○ A. "She's about to step onto a hot stove."

   ● B. "You have only seconds to act."

   ○ C. "Your timing is perfect and she's safe."

   ○ D. "Then it orders your muscles to do so."

3. **Part A**

   Why is your brain considered the control center of your body?

   ○ A. Because it weighs three pounds.

   ○ B. Because exercise can help you solve problems.

   ○ C. Because there are 100 billion neurons in your brain.

   ● D. Because the brain controls everything that your body does.

   **Part B**

   Select two details that **best** support your answer in Part A.

   ☐ A. "You carry around a three-pound mass of wrinkly material in your head that controls every single thing you will ever do." (paragraph 1)

   ☐ B. "So if you're stuck on a homework problem, go out and play a game of soccer, then try the problem again. You just might discover that you're able to solve it." (paragraph 7)

   ☐ C. "Neurons send information to your brain at more than 150 miles (241 kilometers) per hour." (paragraph 4)

   ☒ D. "Accessing the signals coming from your eyes, your brain quickly calculates when, where, and at what speed you will need to dive to intercept her." (paragraph 2)

   ☒ E. "From enabling you to think, learn, create, and feel emotions to controlling every blink, breath, and heartbeat—this fantastic control center is your brain." (paragraph 1)

   ☐ F. "Countless messages zip around inside it every second like a super-charged pinball machine." (paragraph 3)

## Technology-Enhanced Question

**4.** Select the main idea from the text and write it in the box labeled Main Idea. Then select two details that support the main idea. Write each detail in the boxes labeled Supporting Detail 1 and Supporting Detail 2.

**Possible Main Idea**

- The brain is gray, wrinkly, and weighs about three pounds.
- The brain helps you understand what is going on in the world around you.
- Your brain changes as you learn.

**Possible Supporting Details**

- "It is a structure so amazing that a famous scientist once called it 'the most complex thing we have yet discovered in our universe.'" (paragraph 1)
- "Your kitten is on the kitchen counter." (paragraph 2)
- "Neurons send information to your brain at more than 150 miles (241 kilometers) per hour." (paragraph 4)
- "Your brain then uses motor neurons to transmit the message back through your spinal cord to your foot to shake the bee off quickly." (paragraph 5)
- "So if you're stuck on a homework problem, go out and play a game of soccer, then try the problem again." (paragraph 7)
- "No computer can come close to your brain's awesome ability to download, process, and react to the flood of information coming from your eyes, ears, and other sensory organs." (paragraph 2)

**Main Idea**

The main idea is that the story is telling you about how your body worns.

**Supporting Detail 1**

**Supporting Detail 2**

## Technology-Enhanced Question 2

**5.** Select one detail from the list below that goes with each story heading. Write the answers in the boxes.

| Your brain generates enough electricity to power a light bulb. | When you learn, you change the structure of your brain. |
| --- | --- |
| | |

### Details

- "From enabling you to think, learn, create, and feel emotions to controlling every blink, breath, and heartbeat—this fantastic control center is your brain." (paragraph 1)
- "And while a single neuron generates only a tiny amount of electricity, all your neurons together can generate enough electricity to power a low-wattage bulb." (paragraph 3)
- "As you practice, your brain sends 'bike riding' messages along certain pathways of neurons over and over, forming new connections." (paragraph 6)
- "So if you're stuck on a homework problem, go out and play a game of soccer, then try the problem again." (paragraph 7)
- "Accessing the signals coming from your eyes, your brain quickly calculates when, where, and at what speed you will need to dive to intercept her." (paragraph 2)
- "No computer can come close to your brain's awesome ability to download, process, and react to the flood of information coming from your eyes, ears, and other sensory organs." (paragraph 2)

# Answers

1. **Part A: (A); Part B: (B)**

2. **Part A: (B); Part B: (C)**

3. **Part A: (D); Part B: (D) & (E)**

4. The correct answer can be seen below. The best main idea that can be selected is: *The brain helps you understand what is going on in the world around you.* This best summarizes what the story is about. The other two possible main ideas are details in the story. The two best supporting details back up the main idea by showing how the brain interprets information that is occurring around you. These show specific examples. The other details are information provided in the story, but they do not best support the main idea.

---

**Main Idea**

The brain helps you understand what is going on in the world around you.

---

**Supporting Detail 1**

Your brain then uses motor neurons to transmit the message back through your spinal cord to your foot to shake the bee off quickly.

---

**Supporting Detail 2**

No computer can come close to your brain's awesome ability to download, process, and react to the flood of information coming from your eyes, ears, and other sensory organs.

5. The correct answer can be seen below. These details go with each story heading. Some other details seem like they could be correct, but when you refer back to the text you can verify that these details are part of each of these headings.

| Your brain generates enough electricity to power a light bulb. | When you learn, you change the structure of your brain. |
|---|---|
| And while a single neuron generates only a tiny amount of electricity, all your neurons together can generate enough electricity to power a low-wattage bulb. | As you practice, your brain sends "bike riding" messages along certain pathways of neurons over and over, forming new connections. |

## COMMON CORE TIP: READING A VARIETY OF TEXTS

**> For Students:** The Common Core requires that students are able to read literature and informational text. Practice reading a variety of texts at home and at school.

**> For Parents:** Ask your child about what they read, and ask them to support their answer with reasons.

*Literature Example:* What was the theme of the story? How do you know?

*Informational Text Example:* What was the most important detail in the article you read? How do you know?

**> For Teachers:** At least 50% of the text that students read should be informational. Incorporate reading strategies into science and social studies to allow students to apply these skills in the content areas. For example, have students make connections between the social studies text and current events.

# Literary Analysis Task

## Format for the Literary Analysis Task

One unit of the PARCC Assessment is the Literary Analysis Task. You will have ninety minutes to complete this section of the test. In this section of the test, you will be asked to read two literature passages. You will then answer multiple-choice and technology-enhanced questions. Finally, you will be asked to write a literary analysis essay. In this essay, you will have to demonstrate a close reading of the texts. The prompts will ask you to analyze some aspect of the stories and support your analysis with details. When you have completed writing your essay, you will be asked to read  one or more short texts and answer some additional multiple-choice or technology-enhanced questions. Plan to spend about twenty-five minutes reading the passages and answering the multiple-choice and technology-enhanced questions. Then, spend forty-five minutes writing your essay. That will leave you with twenty minutes to read the last text and answer the remaining questions.

For these forty-five minutes, you should balance your time in the following way:

- Ten minutes: prewrite (on your scratch paper)
- Twenty-five minutes: type your first draft
- Ten minutes: edit and revise

  – Read for ideas.
  – Read to add detail.
  – Read to edit spelling and grammar.
  – Read to check for critical components of a strong essay.

There are several different topics that can be the focus of the Literary Analysis PCR. These topics include

- Analysis of structural elements
- Central idea/lesson of the story
- Characters, setting, events
- Author study
- Connecting a text and a related visual

# Before Writing

Before beginning to write, be sure to read through the prompt two or three times to ensure that you understand what is being asked. Make notes on your scrap paper to highlight any key points that you should be sure to include.

As with any type of writing activity, it is vital that you spend time organizing your ideas before beginning. During the prewriting, you can develop a basic outline to guide the direction of your writing. You should spend about ten minutes prewriting on scratch paper. This will help you organize your thoughts.

The nature of this type of essay— explaining and supporting ideas—requires that you prewrite differently than you would a narrative story. It is suggested that you plan five paragraphs: an introduction that includes the main idea, three supporting detail paragraphs, and a concluding paragraph. Organizing your ideas will show the test evaluators that you have a strong command of written language.

When you are planning your writing, be sure to go back into the text and find examples that support your reasons and details. This is an important part of writing a strong literary analysis essay.

# How to Organize Your Response

| Introductory paragraph | Get the attention of the reader with a hook. <br><br> • Ask a question such as "Have you ever wondered?" or "Did you know?" <br> • Use a quote from one of the stories. <br> • Use dialogue and example. Details can really grab your audience. <br><br> State your topic clearly. <br><br> • Avoid using "I" in this sentence. <br><br> Briefly state the main points. <br><br> • Save facts and examples for the detail paragraphs. |
|---|---|

| Detail paragraph—If you want someone to believe it, you must support it. | State your main idea in one clear sentence.<br><br>Explain the idea.<br><br> • Give reasons.<br> • Provide facts.<br> • Use an example of something that happened to you.<br> • Build on details from the stories.<br><br>Vary the way you support your details.<br><br> • Use different beginning words.<br> • Alternate long and short sentences.<br><br>Use transition words.<br><br> • If your details have a chronological order, show that you understand the sequence of events.<br><br>Keep your reader interested! |
|---|---|
| Concluding paragraph | Summarize your main idea (provide support).<br><br> • No new ideas or details are presented here.<br><br>Restate your topic in different words.<br><br>Make a statement about how your feel:<br><br> • Realization of something important.<br> • A lesson that was learned.<br><br>Release or unhook the reader.<br><br> • You may use humor (make the reader think or smile).<br> • One type of ending could be: "The moral of the story is…"<br> • Circle back to the beginning. |

After spending time organizing and writing your work, you should spend the last ten minutes revising and editing your work.

Spend the first five minutes rereading what you have written to make sure that your ideas make sense.

Spend the next three minutes rereading to identify any mechanical errors. These include spelling, punctuation, and capitalization. Finally, spend the last two minutes working to improve the language in the story. Add descriptive words, strong verbs, and expressive vocabulary to make your writing more sophisticated.

Any edits that need to be made should be corrected on your typed draft. Use the backspace key or the cut feature to remove any obvious errors and replace them with corrections. You can also use the copy and paste feature of the editor to move around paragraphs and sentences.

During the final minutes, read through your work one last time to **make sure that everything makes sense**. Go back to the **writer's checklist** and the original prompt, and be sure that you have included all the points listed.

Remember:

- Begin writing and keep writing!
- Edit spelling and punctuation only after all your ideas are on paper.
- Include your best ideas and supporting details from your prewriting.
- Be sure to answer each point in the prompt.
- Be sure to provide examples and details from the stories in your writing.

Now that you have some guidelines to use, try the sample prompt. You should refer to the scoring rubric found in the Appendix before you begin. Try to imitate actual test-taking conditions as closely as possible. Time yourself. Try using the guidelines above to structure your work. When you have finished, use your writer's checklist to ensure that your writing is the best it can be.

# Writer's Checklist

☐ Keep the central idea or topic in mind.

☐ Keep your audience in mind.

☐ Support your ideas with details, explanations, and examples from the text.

☐ State your ideas in a clear sequence.

☐ Include an opening and a closing.

☐ Use a variety of words and vary your sentence structure.

☐ State your conclusion clearly.

☐ Capitalize, spell, and use punctuation correctly.

# GUIDED PRACTICE—LITERARY ANALYSIS TASK

Read the excerpts from *Cheddar's Tales: Crisis in Crittertown*. Then write an essay based on the prompt that follows. After the question is a sample response that shows one possible example of how the question can be answered. A sample of the prewriting is also included.

**Excerpts from *Cheddar's Tales***

*Crisis in Crittertown*

by Justine Fontes

## The Change

1   Before The Change, my thoughts were few and simple: Don't get killed. Find food—hopefully cheese!

2   Back then I didn't even know what cheese was. I just liked to eat it more than anything else. I didn't know what a cow was, and I certainly had no clue about the chemicals that transform milk into the world's greatest food.

3   My knowledge barely reached beyond the basement of the post office in Crittertown, Maine, where my colony and I struggled to keep one jump ahead of hunger, cold, cats, brooms, and other disasters. People and all their amazing inventions meant only two things to us: food and danger. Then suddenly, one October day, everything changed.

4   The music started making sense. That's what I remember first. Music always sounded nice. But then there was that magical morning, when the songs on the radio suddenly had lyrics I could understand. It wasn't just mood and beat. The words made sense!

**5** Everyone else in the colony felt it, too. Our minds sprang to life with words and ideas. We wondered what was happening! Was it only happening to us or to mice everywhere? Then a cricket chirped, "What's going on?" We wondered if it was happening to every critter.

**6** Thanks to birds, word of The Change spread quickly. Birds get around and they gossip. The birds said it was occurring all around human talking machines, like telephones, radios, and TVs. No critter knew why. We only knew that suddenly we understood human babble—and there was a lot of it!

**7** Most of us felt like we'd snapped awake during a thrilling movie that might end in a happily-ever-after or a terrible tragedy. And we weren't just watching the movie. We were characters with an important part to play.

**8** Before The Change, mice didn't have names. We knew each other by smell, sight, and relationships. After it, we quickly came up with names for ourselves—or each other.

**9** Every mouse called me Cheddar because I'm crazy for cheese, especially that sharp, tangy delight known as cheddar. My best friend is the grandson of our leader, and his father is a handsome shade of gray. Therefore, my friend became Grayson. Maybe he'll grow into that dignified name someday. The Grayson I know is a hothead, always rushing into danger.

**10** The morning of The Change was no different. As soon as we realized we could understand humans, Grayson squeaked, "We must explore! Let's go upstairs and find out what they do at the post office."

**11**  Up until then we didn't know zip about zip codes. All we knew about the postal service was when the workers came and went, and what they left in the trash cans.

**12**  "No one's going anywhere!" our leader squeaked firmly. Brownback was a cautious mouse. Like his son, he was mostly gray, but with a stripe of brown down his back. His muzzle fur was white with age. We all respected him greatly—except Grayson.

**13**  "Ah, Pops! There's so much to learn. It could benefit the colony. I'll be careful," Grayson promised. "I won't make a sound or let anyone see me. I'll . . . even take Cheddar along."

**14**  To my surprise, this last phrase changed Brownback's expression.

**15**  Grayson saw that, too, because he squeaked on. "He'll keep me in line. You know Cheddar. He's always holding me back from fun . . . I mean danger."

**16**  Brownback nodded. "Cheddar is cautious, and caution keeps a mouse alive."

**17**  I felt flattered. "Cautious" sounds so much better than "coward."

**18**  Grayson seized on this. "We won't stay long. We'll come home with lots of news for you."

**19**  Brownback always said, "Facts help a leader make good decisions." He liked news almost as much as I like cheese. Brownback nodded. "You and Cheddar may go upstairs."

**20**  Grayson jumped so high, even his tail left the ground.

**21**  Brownback sighed. "Calm down, boy." Then he told me, "Don't let him do anything foolish."

**22**  I nodded, suddenly realizing what had happened. What happened?! When had I agreed to go upstairs?

**The Journey**

**23**   This was even scarier than the time Grayson talked me into helping him use a pencil to trip a trap. I shuddered at that memory. How did I let him get me into these things?

**24**   The first part of our journey was familiar. Grayson and I often visited the parking lot shared by the post office and the Crittertown Market. But we always did this at night when there were no cars or trucks zooming around.

**25**   We watched the cars come and go. How busy everything was during the day!

**26**   People carried bags out of the market, and packages to or from the post office. I squeaked, "They buy food at the market. What do they do at the post office?"

**27**   "Let's find out!" Grayson replied. Then he slid under the torn rubber trim at the bottom of the post office's rickety back door.

**28**   I looked around the parking lot. Staying there alone was almost as scary as following Grayson. Besides, I'd promised Brownback to keep both eyes on his grandson. I scurried under the door after my friend.

**29**   We caught our breath in the back room with the coats. We sniffed and listened. I smelled the postmaster's coffee and the clerk's perfume. I heard the radio playing the "morning mix" of love songs, news, and trivia.

**30**   Grayson tapped my shoulder and then slinked into the office itself. What choice did I have? Once again, I followed my friend into unknown danger.

**31**   Looking around, I found I could read human writing! Posters urged the mail carriers to "Buckle up for safety" and "Watch out for children! School is open."

**32**   "What's school?" I asked.

**33**   Grayson shrugged.

**34** Slowly some things started making sense. Mail turned out to be letters, catalogs, magazines, and packages. Packages contained all kinds of things: big, small, valuable, and some "just old baby clothes I'm sending to my sister."

**35** Grayson and I gradually grasped the postal basics. Workers delivered mail to the people of Crittertown and sent mail from Crittertown to humans elsewhere. Some of those places were very far away.

**36** Before long, Grayson and I felt stuffed with facts. How could we remember them all?

**37** I suggested, "Let's report to your grandfather."

**38** Grayson argued, "Let's learn more."

**39** So we stayed until the mail carriers left on their routes. The carriers were the people who drove the mail to all the homes and businesses in Crittertown.

**40** We watched the postmaster do his morning reports on the computer. Grayson crept closer to find out what this machine did. He whispered, "It sends messages. It records and calculates numbers."

**41** Numbers counted how much you had of something, and they were used in addresses, like the 1, 2, 3, third house on Berry Lane.

**42** I felt smart, but also hungry. "Can't we go home?"

**43** Grayson looked annoyed. "Don't you want to see the rest of the post office? Didn't you hear the Clerk mention the snack table?"

**44** Grayson knew me too well. While the postmaster stared at his computer, we slinked to the front of the office.

**45** I couldn't smell cheese, but I sensed its presence. Maybe cheese sends out a frequency, like a TV broadcast. Maybe my stomach is tuned to the cheese channel.

**46**   Grayson and I scrambled up a stack of Priority Mail boxes to the tabletop. We saw a heap of plastic-wrapped treasures labeled cheese sandwich crackers. My mouth watered and my gut growled. "We shouldn't," I cautioned.

**47**   Grayson chuckled. "We shouldn't, but we will and you know it!"

**48**   While the postmaster talked on the phone, we eased open the nearest package. Oh, that wonderful smell! Grayson tugged the top cracker out of the wrapper. By the time we finished that first orange disk, I decided the post office was the greatest place in the world!

**49**   Grayson wanted to stay all day. But I convinced him to leave when Mike went to lunch. I said, "We can come back tomorrow. This way, Brownback will see you're being cautious." Then I added, "If we stay too long, every mouse will worry and Brownback might not let us out again." That did it. We slipped under the door and into the parking lot and headed home.

**50**   Our nervous friend, Twitchy, spotted us first. He squeaked, "They're here!"

**51**   Twitchy sniffed our noses and then squealed. "It's really you! You're okay!"

**52**   Brownback stepped forward. "I was just starting to worry."

**53**   I winked at Grayson. He winked back.

## Literary Analysis Prompt

**Question:** You have read two stories about the mice that live in the Crittertown Post Office. In this story, the two main characters, Grayson and Cheddar, go on adventures. Write an essay describing Grayson and Cheddar. For each character described,

- Explain how the thoughts, words, and/or actions of the character help you understand what the character is like.
- Explain how the personalities of the characters impact the plot of the story.
- Be sure to include specific details from each story to support your ideas.

## Sample Response

The next section gives you an example of one possible response to this prompt. It will explain how the practice work written here represents the type of literary analysis described in the rubric and prompt. Remember, this is just one example of what good writing looks like.

Read the writing task carefully. Ask yourself:

- What is my topic?
- How can I grab the attention of my reader?
- What are the three main points that I wish to write about?
- What supporting details can I include for each?
- How can I tie these ideas together?
- How can I end with a bang? What is my strong ending?

## Sample Prewriting

| Topic | |
|---|---|
| Cheddar and Grayson have different personalities that impact the plot of the story. | |

| Main Idea | Details |
|---|---|
| Cheddar is responsible and makes good decisions. | • The leader picks Cheddar to keep Grayson in line.<br>• Cheddar tells Grayson to go back home.<br>• He keeps promises even when scared. |
| Grayson is excitable and sometimes does not think things through. | • Grayson rushes to go to the post office.<br>• He was not scared to run through the cars in the parking lot.<br>• Grayson takes risks in the post office. |
| Together the mice make a good team. | • Cheddar keeps Grayson safe.<br>• Grayson encourages Cheddar to do new things.<br>• Cheddar and Grayson are able to bring information back to the colony. |

| Conclusion | |
|---|---|
| The story would be very different if Cheddar and Grayson did not work as a team. | |

## Sample Response

Children are often taught to use the buddy system when swimming. Never swim alone, and always have someone that can help you if you get into trouble while in the water. The same buddy system is seen in the excerpts from "Crisis in Crittertown." In the story, Cheddar and Grayson work together as a team. Each mouse has their own personality, which impacts that plot of the story. Both mice are very different. Cheddar is responsible and makes good decisions, while Grayson is excitable and doesn't always think things through. Together, they make a strong team and are able to help their colony learn about the humans around them.

Cheddar is a responsible mouse who makes good decisions. He is picked by Brownback to go with Grayson to the post-office because Brownback thinks he will keep Grayson safe. Brownback said, "Cheddar is cautious, and caution keeps a mouse alive." When Cheddar and Grayson go upstairs, Cheddar is scared and wants to go back to the colony, but he remembers his promise to Brownback. Even though he is scared, he follows Grayson into the post-office. In the end of the second story, Grayson wants to stay upstairs longer to find out more information, but Cheddar thinks through the situation and urges Grayson to go back downstairs. He says that if they go back, the other mice will be less worried and they will be able to go out again in the future.

Unlike Cheddar, Grayson is impulsive and excitable. He does not think carefully about his decisions. In the story, right after the change, Grayson wants to rush upstairs to see the post-office and learn about the people. When he is allowed upstairs, he dashes across the parking lot without thinking about the possibility that he could be hit by a car. In the post-office, he took other risks as well. He stayed for a long time, took food from the snack table and got close to the humans.

Although both of the mice are very different, they work well together. Cheddar probably wouldn't go upstairs if it weren't for Grayson, and Brownback wouldn't have let Grayson go without Cheddar. Because of Grayson, the mice are able to get information about the humans and understand how the world works. Grayson also helps Cheddar do new things. Cheddar gets to eat new snacks, and learn new things because of it. Cheddar keeps Grayson safe in the story.

This story would be very different if Cheddar and Grayson didn't work together as a team. Without each other, Cheddar might have stayed with the colony, and they would never have learned about the humans. Grayson might have gotten hurt when he searched for the humans, or worse, the humans might have discovered that the mice live in the building. The personalities of the mice are important to the plot of the story. The buddy system is important for children, and mice!

## Evaluation of a Sample Response

After spending time organizing and writing your work, you should spend the last ten minutes revising and editing your work.

Spend the first five minutes rereading what you have written to make sure that your ideas make sense.

### Did you state your main idea in the introductory paragraph?

The main idea of the essay is clearly stated in the introductory paragraph, *"Together, they make a strong team and are able to help their colony learn about the humans around them."* The remainder of the essay focuses on explaining this point.

### Does each of the next paragraphs support the main idea with details?

The rest of the paragraphs support this main idea. Paragraph two and three explain the personality of each of the mice. The third paragraph explains how they work together as a team.

### Does the piece have a single focus?

Yes. The piece is focused on explaining how the personalities of the mice impact the plot of the story.

### Did you include a strong opening and closing sentence?

The writer uses opening and closing sentences that relate the actions of the mice to the actions of humans. Making a connection between mice and humans helps to draw the reader in. This activates the readers' background knowledge about the buddy system and helps them to understand how this might apply to the mice.

### Did you include evidence and examples from the text?

Several quotes from the story and examples are used throughout the essay.

### Did you answer all parts of the question?

The prompt asked the writer to compose an essay that describes the mice and how their personalities impact the plot. The essay answers all points of this question.

Spend the next two minutes rereading to identify mechanical errors. These include spelling, punctuation, and capitalization. Finally, spend the last three minutes working to improve the language in the story. Add descriptive words, strong verbs, and expressive vocabulary to make your writing more sophisticated.

Any edits that need to be made should be corrected on your typed draft. Use the backspace key or the cut feature to remove any obvious errors and replace them with corrections. You can also use the copy and paste feature of the editor to move around paragraphs and sentences.

During the final minutes, read through one last time to **make sure that everything makes sense**. Go back to the **writer's checklist** as well as the original prompt, and be sure that you have included all the points listed.

# INDEPENDENT PRACTICE—LITERARY ANALYSIS TASK

You are now ready to move on to some independent practice of the skills that we have just reviewed. In the pages that follow, you will find two additional stories to read. There are two practice prompts associated with these stories. Be sure to use a timer when you write—plan to spend about sixty minutes writing, and practice typing your response on the computer to help you prepare for the PARCC.

*Puss in Boots is the servant of Marquis. He is a clever cat who is friends with the King.*

### Excerpt from *Puss in Boots: The Watermill*

## Retold by Stella Gurney

1   Once there lived an old miller and his three sons. Their watermill sat on a beautiful river that wound its way through a wealthy kingdom.

2   Each day, with the help of his sons, the miller would work the mill, hefting and grinding the barley and loading the donkeys. But as he grew older, he became frail and tired. He worked less and less until one day, he took to his bed and called his sons to gather around.

3   To the eldest, the miller said, *"John, you have always been a good boy and have worked hard. You shall have the mill when I am gone. You will earn a good living from it."*

4   To his middle son, he said, *"Thomas, you too have always worked hard and have helped your father. You shall have the donkeys—you can hire them out for the harvest each autumn."*

5   Then he turned to his third and youngest son, Peter, and shook his head.

6   *"As for you, my child, you're not a bad boy, but you're lazy. If I left you the mill, you'd let it run to ruin, and I couldn't be sure you'd feed those poor donkeys. I have nothing left to give you, save for . . . "*

**7**   The old man cast his eye around the room and spotted the mill cat, snoozing by the fireside. *"You can have the cat!"* he said at last, satisfied. And with that, he took his final breath.

**8**   The three young men greatly mourned their father's death, but none more so than Peter.

**9**   *"What am I to do?"* he cried. *"How am I to earn a living, with only a useless cat to feed? Thomas, John,"* he turned beseechingly to his brothers. *"Will you allow me to stay here and work for you to earn my living?"*

**10**   But his brothers scoffed. *"We have seen your idea of work, Peter—it is to sit around all day playing your harmonica and idling. No,"* they said firmly. *"You'll have to make your own way in the world."*

**11**   Poor Peter was left alone by the fire with the cat. He sat and stroked its ears, talking idly as he stared into the flames. *"Well Puss, here we are,"* he sighed. *"You're all that stands between me and starvation. Goodness knows what I shall do for food and warmth once I have eaten you and made a soft muff from your fur."*

**12**   Puss raised an eyebrow at Peter's words, but he knew they were only meant in jest. Lazy and foolish his young master may be, but he had always been kind to animals.

**13**  As for the future, Puss knew he could continue to live very well at the mill—catching mice and snoozing by the fire—but perhaps there was more to life. Besides, Puss was fond of Peter and it was clear that Peter needed his help.

**14**  Fortunately, Puss was no ordinary cat. He could talk and think as well as any human being. So Puss pondered over the problem of Peter's livelihood. His new master wasn't keen on hard work—but who in this world gets money for doing nothing, except for kings and noblemen? A-ha! A slow grin spread across Puss's face as the beginnings of an idea took shape.

**15**  *"Young sire,"* he purred to Peter. *"Do not worry. I know exactly how we shall feed and clothe you—and more besides."*

**16**  *"My goodness! You do?"* gasped Peter in astonishment.

**17**  *"I do,"* Puss replied. *"And I ask of you only two things. First, that you trust me always and do exactly as I say."*

**18**  *"And second,"* Puss continued, *"that you give me your finest pair of boots."* (Cats are notoriously vain, and Puss was no exception.)

**19**  Peter was taken aback, but he had no ideas of his own. Having witnessed Puss's tricks for hunting mice in the past, he thought that the cat was as likely as he to come up with a good plan. *"Very well!"* he declared. *"I place my trust in you, Puss. Take my best boots and good luck!"*

### Excerpt from *Puss in Boots: The Marquis*
Retold by Stella Gurney

**1**  One day, as Puss was taking his leave of Court, he overheard a courtier order the royal carriage to be prepared, as the King and the Princess Hermione wished to take a trip along the river.

**2**  This was just the opportunity Puss had been waiting for! He hurried back to the mill to find Peter, whose brothers had grudgingly agreed he could stay for a while, but only until he found a job.

**3**    Sure enough, there was his master, pushing dirt around the mill floor with a broom. He looked up when Puss came in and frowned petulantly.

**4**    *"There you are, you pesky creature,"* growled Peter. *"When am I going to see this plan of yours come good, eh? Every day, my brothers ask when I'll be leaving. I can't keep making up excuses! You told me to trust you, but so far you've done nothing. Nothing!"*

**5**    *"Do not fret, master,"* soothed the cat. *"All is in hand—the plan is ready to be carried out this minute."* Peter grumbled a little but Puss continued to explain: *"I have discovered from a friendly otter that says the water a little farther down the river holds magical powers. Those who swim naked in it find riches and fortune beyond their wildest dreams. There is only one condition . . . "* Here Puss lowered his voice to a dramatic whisper: *"For the magic to work, you must never breathe a word of it to another living soul."*

**6**    *"My goodness!"* exclaimed Peter, eyes wide in wonder. *"Magic water, eh? Amazing—I have lived here all my life and never heard of that! Well, what are we waiting for?"* he cried, beginning to pull off his clothing. *"Finish that sweeping for me, will you, Puss? My fortune awaits!"*

**7**    Within a very short time, Peter was to be found without a stitch on, splashing and thrashing around in a pool downriver from the mill. All the while, Puss stood on the bank, his ears pricked for the sound of the King's carriage. Whatever did that crafty cat have in mind?

**8**    Puss didn't have long to wait before he saw the King's golden carriage in the distance, glinting in the afternoon sun as it rolled along the riverside toward them.

**9**    Darting behind a nearby bush, Puss waited until the carriage drew closer, then leapt out in front of it, waving his hat and crying, *"Help! Help! My master, the Marquis of Carabas, is drowning!"*

**10**    At once, two of the guards dismounted, weapons at the ready to defend their King—bandits were not unknown in these parts. But the

King, leaning out of his window, recognized Puss, and called to his men to stay their arms.

**11** *"Puss in Boots!"* he exclaimed. *"Whatever is the matter?"*

**12** *"Your Majesty,"* gasped Puss breathlessly. *"Thank goodness! My master and I have been attacked by a brutal gang of robbers. The Marquis bravely tried to defend us, but they were too many and have thrown him in the river half-conscious, taking all his belongings and fine clothes."*

**13** *"Heavens!"* cried the King. *"Yes, I see him down there thrashing around. Quick, men—rescue his Lordship at once!*

**14** The guards dashed down to the water's edge and dove right in. Meanwhile, Peter had been so busy splashing in his magic river that he hadn't even noticed the commotion. He was most surprised to find himself being towed back to the riverbank by two burly soldiers.

**15** On the shore, the King and his daughter waited anxiously. *"My dear Marquis, what a dreadful affair!"* exclaimed the King, stepping forward to throw his own cloak around the dripping fellow.

**16** Peter gulped when he recognized his ruler, then looked around to see who the King could possibly be speaking to.

**17** *"You seem unhurt, thank goodness,"* continued the King. *"I must say, I am delighted to finally meet the honorable Marquis of Carabas, even under such regrettable circumstances."*

**18** Peter was struck dumb with wonder. Clearly, the King was talking to *him*! The magic river had turned him into a Marquis, no less—a nobleman! At last, the life he'd always deserved was his! Throwing back his shoulders, Peter gave a deep, flourishing bow. *"Your Majesty,"* he crooned, before being ushered toward the King's fine carriage by the blushing Princess Hermione.

## Literary Analysis Question 1

**Question:** You have read a story about the Puss in Boots and the Marquis. In this story, the two main characters, Puss in Boots and the Marquis are working together to play a trick. Write an essay that describes the trick.

- Explain who Puss and the Marquis are trying to trick, and why.
- Explain how the trick was played and if it was successful.
- Be sure to include specific details from each story to support your ideas.

-------------------------------------------------------------

-------------------------------------------------------------

-------------------------------------------------------------

-------------------------------------------------------------

-------------------------------------------------------------

-------------------------------------------------------------

-------------------------------------------------------------

-------------------------------------------------------------

-------------------------------------------------------------

-------------------------------------------------------------

-------------------------------------------------------------

-------------------------------------------------------------

-------------------------------------------------------------

## Literary Analysis Question 2

**Question:** You have just read two stories called "The Watermill" and "The Marquis." All stories have a problem and a solution. Often, there are steps taken to solve the problem. Write an essay that identifies the problem, provides steps to solve the problem, and proposes a solution in the story.

- Identify one problem and solution from the stories.
- Explain the steps taken to solve the problem.
- Be sure to include specific details from each story to support your ideas.

---

---

---

---

---

---

---

---

---

---

---

---

---

------------------------------------------------------------

------------------------------------------------------------

------------------------------------------------------------

------------------------------------------------------------

------------------------------------------------------------

------------------------------------------------------------

------------------------------------------------------------

------------------------------------------------------------

------------------------------------------------------------

------------------------------------------------------------

------------------------------------------------------------

------------------------------------------------------------

------------------------------------------------------------

------------------------------------------------------------

------------------------------------------------------------

------------------------------------------------------------

------------------------------------------------------------

## COMMON CORE TIP: LITERARY ANALYSIS

**> For Students:** Texts come in a variety of genres. A genre is a type of text. Some genres include biography, realistic fiction, fantasy, and personal narrative. When you select a book to read, try to identify the genre of the book before you begin reading it.

**> For Parents:** Practice analyzing TV shows that you watch with your child (sitcoms). Talk about the problem and solution in the episode. Compare one show to another, and talk about how they are alike or different. Discuss the characters' actions in the show.

**> For Teachers:** Teach about genre, elements of plot (setting, character, theme, conflict, solution, etc.), and literary devices (simile, metaphor, onomatopoeia, personification, idioms, hyperbole, and alliteration) to assist students in writing their literary analysis.

# CHAPTER 4

# Research Simulation Task

## Format for the Research Simulation Task

The Research Simulation Task is designed to require students to analyze a topic that is presented through informational text and/or multimedia. You will read an anchor text, which will introduce the topic, and then read/view two additional texts/media. To help students fully engage in the texts, multiple-choice and technology-enhanced questions will be presented. You will also write an analytical essay that will synthesize information from the sources presented in this section of the test.

You will have ninety minutes to complete this portion of the test. You should plan to spend twenty-five minutes reading and reviewing the sources included in this section. There are approximately eight multiple-choice and technology-enhanced questions. Plan to spend about twenty minutes answering these questions. This will give you approximately forty-five minutes to write your essay.

In your essay, your task is to examine a topic and convey information clearly in response to the prompt. The essay should be well organized and include paragraphs. The topic should be developed with facts, definitions, concrete details, quotations, and/or examples. Ideas should be linked with transition words. Be sure to use precise language and include a conclusion to your writing.

The research simulation task will focus on one of two skills. The first skill is analyzing the role of illustrations in the text. This might include interpreting information that is presented in charts, graphs, timelines, etc. and explaining how the information helps the reader to understand the text. The second possible skill focus is analyzing the relationship between a series of concepts. In a task with this focus, you will need to explain events, procedures, ideas, or concepts as related to the texts read. In addition, both texts will require you to refer to details and examples from multiple texts.

# Before Writing

Before beginning to write, be sure to read through the prompt two or three times to ensure that you understand what is being asked. Make notes on your scrap paper to highlight any key points that you should be sure to include.

As with any type of writing activity, it is vital that you spend time organizing your ideas before beginning. During the prewriting, you can develop a basic outline to guide the direction of your writing. You should spend about fifteen minutes prewriting on scratch paper. This will help you organize your thoughts.

This type of writing requires that you make a claim and support it with examples and details from multiple sources. In order to prewrite for the research simulation task, you will need to determine the following components:

- Claim: Identify the claim that you will make in your essay. This is the topic of your essay and the argument that you will support.
- Subheadings: Develop subheadings for your essay. The subheadings are the individual topics that support your claim.
- Notes: Write notes under each subheading. These notes should include details, examples, quotes, etc. that come from the sources that you have read or viewed.

You should create one box for each of your subheadings with space to take notes underneath. The example on the next page shows a graphic organizer suitable for an essay that will contain three subheadings.

# Prewriting

| Major Claim: | | |
| --- | --- | --- |
| | | |

| Subheading 1: | Subheading 2: | Subheading 3: |
| --- | --- | --- |
| Notes: | Notes: | Notes: |
| | | |

# How to Organize Your Response

After you complete your prewriting, you will need to write your response. The table below explains how you can organize your response. This is similar to the structure used in the Literary Analysis Task.

| | |
|---|---|
| **Introductory paragraph** | Get the attention of the reader with a hook.<br><br>• Ask a question such as, "Have you ever wondered?" or "Did you know?"<br>• Use a quote from one of the stories.<br>• Use dialogue— explanations can really grab your audience.<br><br>State your topic claim clearly.<br><br>Briefly state the subheadings in a few sentences.<br><br>• Save facts and examples for the detail paragraphs. |
| **Detail paragraph** | Write at least one paragraph for each of your subheadings. Sometimes you might write two or three paragraphs for each subheading.<br><br>State the topic.<br><br>Support the topic.<br><br>• Give reasons.<br>• Provide facts.<br>• Use an example of something that happened to you.<br>• Build on details from the stories.<br><br>Vary the way you support your details.<br><br>• Use different beginning words.<br>• Alternate long and short sentences.<br><br>Use transition words.<br><br>• If your details have a chronological order, show that you understand the sequence of events.<br><br>Keep your reader interested! |

| **Concluding paragraph** | Restate your claim in different words. |
| --- | --- |
| | • No new ideas or details are presented here. |
| | Make a statement that shows something important to the claim. |
| | Release or unhook the reader. |
| | • You may use humor (make the reader think or smile).<br>• Circle back to the beginning.<br>• Provide closure. |

After spending time organizing and writing, you should spend the last ten minutes revising and editing your work.

Spend the first five minutes rereading what you have written to make sure that your ideas make sense.

Spend the next three minutes rereading to identify any mechanical errors. These include spelling, punctuation, and capitalization. Finally, spend the last two minutes working to improve the language in your story. Add descriptive words, strong verbs, and expressive vocabulary to make your writing more sophisticated.

Any edits that need to be made should be corrected on your typed draft. Use the backspace key or the cut feature to remove any obvious errors and replace them with corrections. You can also use the copy and paste feature of the editor to move around paragraphs and sentences.

During the final minutes, read through your work one last time to **make sure that everything makes sense**. Go back to the **writer's checklist** and the original prompt, and be sure that you have included all the points listed.

Remember:

- Begin writing and keep writing!
- Edit spelling and punctuation only after all your ideas are on paper.
- Include your best ideas and supporting details from your prewriting.
- Be sure to answer each point in the prompt.
- Be sure to provide examples and details from the sources in your writing.

Now that you have some guidelines to use, try the sample prompt. Refer to the writing rubric found in Appendix A before you begin. Try to imitate actual test-taking conditions as closely as possible. Time yourself. Try using the guidelines above to structure your work. When you have finished, use your writer's checklist to ensure that your writing is the best it can be.

## Writer's Checklist

☐ Keep the central idea or topic in mind.

☐ Keep your audience in mind.

☐ Support your ideas with details, explanations, and examples from the text.

☐ State your ideas in a clear sequence.

☐ Include an opening and a closing.

☐ Use a variety of words and vary your sentence structure.

☐ State your conclusion clearly.

☐ Capitalize, spell, and use punctuation correctly.

# GUIDED PRACTICE—RESEARCH SIMULATION TASK

Read the articles about surviving in the wilderness. There are two articles and one table included as sources for the task. Then write an essay based on the prompt that follows. After the question is a sample response that shows one possible example of how the question can be answered. A sample of the prewriting is also included.

## Lost! Survival in the Wilderness

1    What if you were walking in the woods alone and got lost? What would you do? When you realize that you are lost, you might start to panic. Take a deep breath and stop. Think about what is happening and observe your surroundings. Once you have thought about the problem, create a plan to stay safe.

2    The most important thing to do is to stay in one place. If you are lost, it will be hard to find your way out. As soon as someone realizes that you are missing, they will begin a search. If you stay in one place, it will be much easier for someone to find you. It also reduces the risk of you being injured. If you are with a group of people, be sure to stay together.

3    The most important things that you need to do while waiting for rescue is to maintain your body temperature, conserve energy, drink water, and attract attention (if possible).

4    You can maintain your body temperature in different ways. If it is cold, you need to stay warm. You can find shelter, use a blanket, etc. Trees can help break the wind or protect you from snow or rain. If it is hot, look for shade to stay cool.

5    Your body will need water more than it needs food. Look for water around where you are lost. Drinking from a spring is generally safe. If you are going to drink from a river or pond, it is best to boil the water for at least 10 minutes before you drink it. This will only work if you are able to build a fire. If you cannot build a fire, you can strain the water through your shirt or some other material. This

will help remove anything that might make you sick. A final option is to collect rainwater or morning dew as drinking water.

6    Finally, it is important to attract attention if you can. Carrying a whistle is important when you are going out into the wilderness. A whistle is an effective signaling tool that will help searchers find you. Three short blasts is a known signal for help. In addition, try using rocks, branches, or sticks to draw an X or an SOS on the ground. If you hear a helicopter, wave your arms. Hold a flag or bright-colored fabric in your hand to help anyone see you from the air.

7    The best way to stay safe if you become lost in the wilderness is to prepare before you go. Let someone know where you are going, and when you expect to return. Water, a brightly colored bandana, and a flashlight are also important tools to have. A few garbage bags in your pack can also be used as a blanket, a tarp, or a water collection device. Matches and a pocket knife can also be helpful additions to your pack.

8    Getting lost can be scary. It is important to remember these survival tips and to stay calm. Find water, seek shelter, and stay in one place. If you follow these tips, and prepare before you go, rescue should come and you will stay safe.

**Survival Essentials**

---

> **This article contains safety information about going on an expedition in the wilderness.**

---

**9   Water:** You need water to survive, but beware. Water from streams and rivers could be polluted and make you ill. You must boil it before you drink it.

**10   Protein:** Your muscles need protein to make them strong. Meat, eggs, cheese, and nuts are good sources of protein.

**11   Carbohydrates:** Your body needs sugar for energy, and it gets it from carbohydrates. Rice and pasta are good to eat before an expedition. Grain bars are great snacks.

**12**   Never eat something you don't recognize. Lots of plants, berries, and fungi (mushrooms) are poisonous.

**13**   Wild animals might be unwelcome companions on an expedition, but you can't really blame them. After all, you're in their territory!

## ANIMAL SURVIVAL TIPS

- Blow a whistle if you're walking in bear country. *Why? Bears avoid loud noises.*

- Don't suck the poison out of someone else's snake bite. *Why? The poison may work on you.*

- If you get bitten by a poisonous animal, keep still while you wait for help. *Why? Moving makes poison flow faster through your body.*

- Avoid animals with their young. *Why? They may attack to protect their babies.*

- If you meet a grizzly bear, climb a tree. *Why? Grizzlies can't climb trees, but remember that black bears can.*

**14**   While on your expedition, you have to be prepared for a range of small but scary critters! Here's a nightmare checklist.

**15**   **Snakes:** There are hundreds of different kinds of poisonous snakes in the world. The most deadly land snakes live in Australia and can kill in minutes.

**16**   **Scorpions:** Scorpions have a stinger in their tail. The most dangerous live in the Sahara Desert in Africa and can cause serious illness. They tend to hide in dark, shadowy places such as shoes and sleeping bags.

**17**   **Spiders:** The world's most poisonous spiders are the funnel-web spiders found in Australia, and the brown recluse spiders found in the U.S. Both can cause serious illness.

**18**   **Parasitic Worms:** A nasty range of tiny parasites can be ingested by unwary travelers who drink or eat contaminated water or food. They live inside the body, and can make their host very ill.

**19**   After that loathsome list, do you still want to go traveling? Before you go, check out what kind of crazy creatures you might face.

**20**   **Expedition Tip:** Creepy crawlies are often timid, and if you don't surprise them, they are less likely to attack.

### How Long Can You Survive Without the Things That You Need?

| Air | 3 minutes |
|---|---|
| Shelter | 3 hours (in harsh weather—snow, cold, rain) |
| Water | 3 days |
| Food | 3 weeks |

## Research Simulation Task

You have read three articles about Survival in the Wilderness, which can be a scary and dangerous experience for someone who becomes stranded in the wilderness.

The three texts are:

- Lost! Survival in the Wilderness
- Survival Essentials
- How Long Can You Survive Without the Things That You Need? (Table)

Write an essay that argues for what you think are the three most important things to consider if you are lost in the wilderness. Be sure to support your argument with claims that are developed with clear reasons and evidence from the texts.

## Sample Prewriting

| **Major Claim** |
|---|
| If you become lost in the wilderness, you need to take a few steps to help stay safe. |

| **Subheading 1**<br>Stay calm and make a plan. | **Subheading 2**<br>Keep your body safe. | **Subheading 3**<br>Attract attention. |
|---|---|---|
| Stay calm.<br><br>Stay in one place.<br><br>Create a plan.<br><br>Is there danger?<br><br>What do you have in your pack that can help you? | Maintain body temperature—find shelter<br><br>Stay cool or warm.<br><br>Find clean fresh water—spring, stream, etc.<br><br>Boil water.<br><br>Collect rainwater or dew.<br><br>Be watchful for animals. | Write SOS.<br><br>Wave your arms.<br><br>Make noise—whistle. |

## Sample Response

How to Stay Safe When You Are Lost

One minute you are happily enjoying the sights and sounds of the forest, and the next minute your heart is racing. Nothing around you looks familiar, and you realize that you are lost in the woods. Questions start racing through your head—What should I do? Will anyone find me? Am I going to be okay? Your heart is pounding, and you are breathing quickly.

Getting lost is scary, but by taking a few steps, you can ensure that you will stay safe while you wait for help to arrive. Before you do anything, you need to stop, take a deep breath, and assess the situation. Sit down, breathe deeply, and look around. What are your surroundings like, and what are the needs that you need to address to stay safe? Staying calm and assessing the situation is the first thing you need to do if you are lost in the wilderness.

Next, you need to address your two most immediate needs— water and maintaining your body temperature. In extreme temperatures, your body can only sustain itself without shelter for a few hours. Think about what the weather is. If it is hot, you need to stay cool. Move to the shade and take off any layers of clothing that are not needed. If it is cold, windy, or rainy, you need to create some kind of shelter to stay warm and dry. Check your pack and see what you might have that you could use to create a shelter. A poncho or garbage bag can help keep you dry. A sweatshirt or hat can help you stay warm.

Your body can go three days without water, but it's important to try and find water as soon as possible. Walk around the immediate area and see if you can find a spring or stream of fresh water. It is best to boil any water that you find in nature because it might contain parasites or bacteria. If you can't boil the water, it might be best to try and collect rainwater to drink. You can use a large leaf, tarp, or plastic bag to collect water. This water should be safe to drink.

While you are in the forest, there will be many animals around you. Most of them will not bother you. If you see a snake or a spider, try to avoid it as some of them are poisonous. If you have a whistle, you can blow it to scare aware bears, and probably other animals as well.

The last thing that you need to do is to try and attract attention to yourself. If you have a whistle, blow it frequently so that people can hear you. You can also write SOS on the ground in large letters. If you hear a helicopter, wave your arms while holding a bright cloth to attract attention. It is important to stay in one place so that the rescuers can find you.

Getting lost can be very scary. Creating a plan, finding water and shelter, and attracting attention to yourself are important steps to take if you become lost. If you can stay safe, it will only be a matter of time before rescuers find you and you are back in your bed safe and sound.

## Evaluation of a Sample Response

After spending time organizing and writing your
work, you should spend the last ten minutes
revising and editing your work.

Spend the first five minutes rereading what you
have written to make sure that your ideas make
sense.

### Did you state your claim in the introduction?

The claim of the essay is stated in the second
paragraph, "*Getting lost is scary, but by taking a
few steps, you can ensure that you will stay safe while you wait for help to arrive.*"
The rest of the essay is focused on supporting this claim by explaining the steps to
stay safe.

### Is the claim supported throughout the essay?

Yes, the claim is supported through three subheadings in the essay. The three
subheadings were determined by the question, which asks for three steps to stay
safe. Each subheading is explained in one to three paragraphs.

### Does the piece have a single focus?

Yes. The essay is focused on supporting the claim and identifying ways that
someone can stay safe when lost in the wilderness.

### Did you include a strong opening and closing?

The writer uses an opening that describes strong feelings. This is done to draw
the readers into the essay and help them visualize how they might feel if lost in
the wilderness. The closing of the essay restates the claim and closes with another
strong sensory detail to connect with the readers.

### Did you include evidence and examples from the text?

Evidence and examples from the sources are used throughout the essay.

## Did you answer all parts of the question?

The prompt asked the writer to compose an essay that identifies three important steps for staying safe in the wilderness. This essay lists those steps and uses examples and details as support.

Spend the next two minutes rereading to identify mechanical errors. These include spelling, punctuation, and capitalization. Finally, spend the last three minutes working to improve the language in the story. Add descriptive words, strong verbs, and expressive vocabulary to make your writing more sophisticated.

Any edits that need to be made should be corrected on your typed draft. Use the backspace key or the cut feature to remove any obvious errors and replace them with corrections. You can also use the copy and paste feature of the editor to move around paragraphs and sentences.

During the final minutes, read through one last time to **make sure that everything makes sense.** Go back to the **writer's checklist** as well as the original prompt, and be sure that you have included all the points listed.

# INDEPENDENT PRACTICE—RESEARCH SIMULATION TASK

Read the articles about animal adaptations and habitats. There are three articles included as sources for the task. There are two prompts that follow the sources. You can practice writing an essay for each of the tasks.

### Animal Adaptations

by Wendie Hensley and Annette Licata

**1**   Just like you, animals have special body parts that help them survive. These body parts are adaptations. Think about some of your favorite animals. What kind of adaptations do they have? Beaks, claws, whiskers, and stripes are physical adaptations. Here are some examples of how animals use their special body parts:

- **Beaks**—Birds use their beaks mainly for eating. An owl will use its sharp beak to tear meat. A parrot will use its strong, curved beak for cracking open nuts.

- **Webbed feet**—Webbed feet are perfect for animals that spend time in the water. They help ducks move easily across a pond. Penguins and otters also have webbed feet to help them swim.

- **Claws**—A squirrel uses its claws for climbing trees. Crabs have a different kind of claw that they use for protection and holding food. Prairie dogs have a sharp set of claws for digging.

- **Eyes**—Placement of an animal's eyes is a special adaptation. Predators, or animals that hunt, such as lions, wolves, and owls, have their eyes on the fronts of their faces to help them find their prey. Prey animals, or animals that are hunted, such as rabbits, deer, and zebras have their eyes on the sides of their faces to watch for danger.

- **Camouflage**—Camouflage is an adaptation that helps an animal hide from other animals. Walking sticks are insects that look like the tree branches they live on. A tiger's stripes help it to hide in the jungle plants so that it can catch other animals. An octopus can change its skin color to look like the rock it is sitting on. The spotted scorpion fish looks like a rock while it sits on the ocean floor waiting for dinner to swim by.

### Animal Habitats and Changes for Survival
by Wendie Hensley and Annette Licata

1   Planet Earth is covered with many types of habitats. Each of those habitats is filled with plants and animals that have special features and behaviors, which help them survive. Here are some examples.

2   Picture this—You're walking across the hot, dry sand of the desert. There's no water or shade. The sun is beating down on your head. Your throat is so dry that you're dreaming of swimming pools and ice-cold lemonade. Your sweat-soaked shirt is sticking to your back. The sand is so hot you can feel it through the bottoms of your shoes. How do you survive here? You'd probably hike back to the motor home and pull a soda out of the ice chest. But if you were a jackrabbit, it wouldn't be so easy.

3   You might think that nothing could survive here, but many plants and animals call this place home. How do they do it? They all have special features and behaviors that help them live in this desert habitat.

4   An average desert gets less than 14 inches of rain per year. The desert has very hot days and very cold nights. It is covered with sand and low growing plants.

### Desert Tortoise

- Special feature—Tortoises have large, thick legs with strong claws that help them dig.

- Special behavior—Tortoises burrow into large holes to keep out of the sun and the cold night air.

### Gila Woodpecker

- Special feature—Woodpeckers have sharp beaks to help them drill holes in a cactus and for catching and eating insects.

- Special behavior—Woodpeckers nest high inside a cool, safe cactus.

### Barrel Cactus

- Special feature—The cactus is covered with sharp spines that protect it from being eaten.

- Special behavior—The cactus likes eating cold pizza for breakfast. Just kidding. Wanted to make sure you were paying attention.

5   Picture this—You're walking through a dark, thick forest where the air is wet and sticky. Your hair and clothes are stuck to your skin. The thick canopy of leaves above you blocks the sunlight. An ant walks over the toe of your shoe, and it is nearly as big your grandma's toy poodle. You have entered the dark green habitat known as the rain forest. And the animals and plants that live in this habitat are amazing. The average rain forest is hot and wet all year long. It has very tall trees that stay green all year. Many plants grow on the forest floor.

### Orangutan

- Special feature—Orangutans have long arms for swinging and climbing.

- Special behavior—Orangutans build their nests up high in trees for safety.

## Tree Frogs

- Special feature—Tree frogs have toes with round pads that make a sticky goo, which helps them climb.

- Special behavior—Tree frogs are nocturnal, which means they are up at night. This helps them hide from predators.

## Lianas

- Special features—Lianas are vines with extra-long roots that help them to climb trees.

- Special behavior—Lianas climb tall trees to reach up through the heavy canopy to find sunlight.

6   Picture this—You're covered from head to toe in warm winter clothes as you walk slowly across slippery ice. Your nose is so frozen that if you sneeze it might break off. You see nothing but an endless sea of white snow and ice. There are no trees and very few living things. You wonder if anything lives here on the tundra. An average tundra is flat with no trees. There is a frozen layer under the ground that never melts.

## Arctic Fox

- Special features—Arctic foxes are covered in thick, white fur even on their ears and the bottoms of their feet. The fur keeps them warm and makes them hard to see in the snow.

- Special behavior—Arctic foxes travel longer distances than any other land animal except humans.

## Puffin

- Special feature—The puffins' thick, waterproof feathers protect them and keep them warm while diving in the ocean.

- Special behavior—Puffins spend a lot of time floating on the ocean surface and cleaning their feathers.

**Arctic Poppy**

- Special feature—The Arctic poppy's cup-shaped flower helps it catch sunlight.

- Special behavior—The poppy flower turns to follow the sun and attract insects to its warm petals.

7   Picture this—You're swimming in the salty water of the ocean. You must keep moving your arms and legs so the waves do not drag you away. Behind every rock, a deadly predator might be hiding ready to make a meal of you. And the deeper you swim, the darker and colder it gets. There are no average oceans. The temperature, sunlight, and salt are different in each ocean.

**Shark**

- Special feature—Sharks have light, soft bones to keep them floating.

- Special behavior—Many sharks hunt by staying very quiet until a fish swims past.

**Clownfish**

- Special feature—Clownfish have bright colors, which attract other fish to swim closer.

- Special behavior—The clownfish make their home in or near the stinging anemone so that predators that swim near are stung.

**Seaweed**

- Special feature—Some types of seaweed have large leaves for catching sunlight.

- Special behavior—Some types of seaweed whip other types of seaweed out of their space.

## A Tail Comes in Handy

1   Animals use their tails for different purposes. You can learn fascinating information about animals just from observing their tails.

2   A tail comes in handy for communication. Animals such as wolves and ostrich use their tails to show rank among the group. A timid wolf will keep its tail between its legs, whereas a fearless wolf will raise its tail. The highest-ranking male ostrich will hold his tail pointing straight up to show his dominance. The next-highest male will hold his tail horizontal, while other birds droop their tails down to show they are subordinate.

3   Deer also use their tails to communicate with each other. A white-tailed deer will lift its tail straight up and wag it, showing the white fur underneath. The white fur acts like an alarm or signal, which warns other deer of approaching danger.

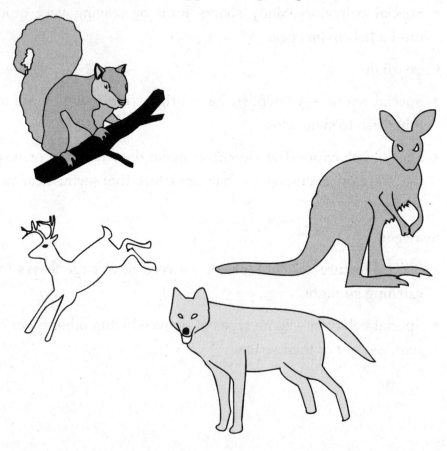

**4**　A tail comes in handy for balance purposes. The kangaroo and the squirrel use their tails for balance. A kangaroo's tail acts like a third leg; it allows the animal to prop itself up. The squirrel's bushy tail not only provides warmth on winter days, but it also helps the animal keep its balance when it is leaping and climbing.

**5**　A tail comes in handy for movement. Birds use their tails to move around and balance on branches. Most fish have tails that help them with movement and direction. A tail comes in handy to scare off predators. Many animals use their tails to give a warning that they feel threatened and are ready to defend themselves. To warn would-be attackers, a rattlesnake will rattle its tail and a porcupine will raise its quills and shake. A ground iguana scares off its enemies by whipping its tail fiercely. Horses, giraffes, cows, and lions have tails that can swat off the peskiest of flies.

**6**　Tails serve many purposes. They can be as useful to animals as a baseball is to a pitcher.

## Research Simulation Task 1

You have read three articles about animal adaptations and different habitats. These adaptations help animals survive in many unique ways.

The three articles are

- Animal Adaptations
- Animal Habitats and Changes for Survival
- A Tail Comes in Handy

Animals use these adaptations to communicate, stay safe, and find food. Write an essay that uses information from the three texts to explain the ways that animals communicate, stay safe, and find food using their adaptations. Be sure to support your argument with claims that are developed with clear reasons and evidence from the texts.

-------------------------------------------------------------------------

-------------------------------------------------------------------------

-------------------------------------------------------------------------

-------------------------------------------------------------------------

-------------------------------------------------------------------------

-------------------------------------------------------------------------

-------------------------------------------------------------------------

-------------------------------------------------------------------------

-------------------------------------------------------------------------

-------------------------------------------------------------------------

## Research Simulation Task 2

You have read three articles about animal adaptations and different habitats. Different habitats require different adaptations.

The three articles are

- Animal Adaptations
- Animal Habitats and Changes for Survival
- A Tail Comes in Handy

Select two habitats that are discussed in the articles. Compare and contrast the habitats, and explain how they are alike and different. Be sure to include the types of adaptations that animals in each habitat need to survive. Support your claims with reasons and evidence from the texts.

---------------------------------------------------------------------

---------------------------------------------------------------------

---------------------------------------------------------------------

---------------------------------------------------------------------

---------------------------------------------------------------------

---------------------------------------------------------------------

---------------------------------------------------------------------

---------------------------------------------------------------------

---------------------------------------------------------------------

---------------------------------------------------------------------

_____

_____

_____

_____

_____

_____

_____

_____

_____

_____

_____

_____

_____

_____

_____

_____

# COMMON CORE TIP: RESEARCH TASK

**> For Students and Parents:** Identify a topic that interests you. It could be an animal, a video game, a sport, or a famous person. Use the Internet, and visit the library to find at least three sources about the topic. A source could be a website, an article, a book, or a video. After you read/view at least three sources, tell your parent or another person what you learned. Parents should help their child find appropriate sources for their research.

**> For Teachers:** Help students organize their research topics. Teach students to identify a topic and then to brainstorm questions that they have about that topic. The questions can then be organized into headings for their research. Create a page for each "heading" so that students can take notes as their read/view sources. Be sure to talk about plagiarism as well to help students understand why taking notes is important.

# CHAPTER 5

# Narrative Writing Task

## Format for the Narrative Writing Task

On the PARCC Assessment one of the units will be the Narrative Writing Task. On the day of the Narrative Writing Task, you will be asked to read a story. Then you will answer four multiple-choice and technology-enhanced questions. After you have answered these questions, you will be asked to complete a Prose Constructed-Response prompt. This task will ask you to write a story that is related to the text that you just read. Then you will be asked to read one or two more texts, and you will answer six more questions.

The Narrative Writing Task may seem challenging. In our everyday ELA classes, we are given much more time to complete the five steps of the writing process: prewriting, writing, revising, editing, and publishing. On this test, you are expected to do all five in a fraction of the time you usually have! In addition, you will need to type your story as you compose it. Therefore, you need to develop a structure that you can practice before the test in order to build your confidence and ability to write this way.

Timed writing to a prompt is a skill that can be developed. You need to keep in mind that your audience is a team of evaluators who are looking for the qualities of good narrative writing. You will be scored on a rubric that is found in Appendix A.

Many fourth-grade teachers have observed that students spend too much time either preparing for writing (prewriting, outlining, making webs) or just jumping into the writing task without a direction or focus. In either case, students do not have enough time to revise or edit and often do not get to finish drafting an ending to the story. As you will see later in the chapter, having strong opening and closing sentences are critical to scoring well on the rubric.

The guideline on page 94 is one possible way to organize your time effectively.

Spend about twenty minutes reading the first passage and answering the multiple-choice and technology-enhanced questions. This will give you forty-five minutes to work on writing your story. For these forty-five minutes, you should balance your time in the following way:

- Five minutes: prewrite (on your scratch paper)
- Thirty minutes: type your first draft
- Ten minutes: edit and revise

  - Read for ideas
  - Read to add detail
  - Read to edit spelling and grammar
  - Read to check for critical components of a good story

This will leave you with twenty-five minutes to read the final selection(s) and answer the remaining questions.

## Prewriting

Without a doubt, your classroom teachers have introduced you to many different ways of organizing your ideas for writing. On the PARCC, you must complete this part of the process quickly. If you use a web or graphic organizer, remember to jot down only key words or phrases about your ideas—NOT complete sentences.

## Some Effective Ways to Organize Your Writing

- Word web
- Beginning, middle, end: On a separate line for each, write the letters B, M, and E on the left side of the page. Follow each letter with a few words or phrases to give the piece direction.

- Story elements: Outline the characters, setting, problem, and solution for your story.
- 5 Ws and 1 H

  1. **WHO** is in the story? (characters, people, animals, objects)

  2. **WHAT** is happening?

  3. **WHEN** is it happening? (can be time of day, time of year, time in history)

  4. **WHERE** is it happening?

  5. **WHY** is it happening?

  6. **HOW** is it happening?

If during this time you get a brainstorm for a wonderful opening or closing sentence, jot it down as well. At first, writing an ending sentence before you have written the story may feel funny, but many students have found that it gives them a direction to aim toward as they write.

Try to take in all the details you know from the story that you read. You may want to think about:

- What happened right before the story/prompt
- What is happening now in the story/prompt
- What you think might happen next

You will be given two sheets of blank scrap paper. You can use these pages to plan your writing. You do not have to use both pages. **DO NOT** write your final answer on these pages as they will not count toward your score. Many students have begun their writing here, thinking that they would have plenty of time to type it on the computer, and then have run out of time! The importance of using this space only for planning cannot be overemphasized.

# Writing the First Draft

Unlike other types of writing you may do, you will be scored on the first draft of your writing (with revisions and editing, of course). In addition, you must type the first draft of your writing. Be sure to keep your story about the prompt.

## Remember the Story Elements

Your story should have a beginning, middle, and end. In the beginning of the story, provide a good opening. In addition, describe the characters and setting in the story. In the middle, introduce the problem in your story. Explain the steps that the character(s) take to solve the problem. At the end of the story, be sure to provide a solution to the problem. Don't forget to include a strong closing sentence as well. The table below explains each of these elements in more detail.

| Characters | Describe the characters in your story. Make them real to your audience by giving them names, ages, and histories. Use your senses to show what the characters see, feel, taste, touch, and smell. Make sure that if something is happening in the prompt, it is happening in your story as well. |
|---|---|
| Setting | Tell when and where your story takes place. |
| Problem | Remember that all good stories have a conflict or problem. Be sure to state what it is. |
| Steps to solve the problem | In order to develop the middle of your story, be sure that the characters take steps to solve the problem in the story. |
| Solution | Present a solution to the problem in the end of the story. |

- During this time, it is important that you **do** begin writing and keep writing. Use all of the time allotted.
- **Don't** interrupt the flow of ideas to correct your spelling or punctuation. You can do that later.
- You **don't** have to include everything you wrote in your prewriting, but **do** be sure to include your best ideas. The content and organization of your writing carries the greatest weight when scoring your essay.
- The mechanics of spelling, grammar, capitalization, and punctuation **do** count and should be reviewed as you will see in the following section on editing.

# Editing

Spend your first five minutes **rereading what you have written** to make sure that your ideas make sense. Consider these questions:

- Do you have a logical beginning, middle, and end?
- Does the piece have a single focus?
- Did you include a strong opening and closing sentence?
- Did you include the important things from your prewriting?

This is the time to change any obvious sentence or paragraph errors. Make sure that you use the proper pronouns and verb tenses. For example, if you have used "ed" in your story to express action in the past, stay in the past throughout your writing.

Spend the next three minutes **identifying mechanical errors**:

- Spelling errors
- Punctuation errors
- Capitalization errors

The third read through during the next three minutes is to **add descriptive language** to your writing.

- Add adjectives to liven up things.
- Replace boring verbs like "said" with stronger ones like "blurted."
- Try using some figurative language such as metaphors and similes.
- Elaborate with new details.

Any edits that need to be made should be corrected on your typed draft. Use the backspace key or the cut feature to remove any obvious errors and replace them with corrections. You can also use the copy and paste feature of the editor to move around paragraphs and sentences.

During the final minutes, read through one last time to **make sure that everything makes sense**. Go back to the **writer's checklist** as well as the original prompt, and be sure that you have included all the points listed.

During the test, your teacher will write the number of minutes remaining on the board, usually in five-minute increments. You will need to monitor yourself and use your time wisely. Be sure that when the time is changed to ten minutes left, you use this time to put the finishing touches on your draft, write your ending, and get ready to edit. With practice, you will get a feel for the time you have.

Now that you have one idea of a framework to use, you are ready to complete Writing Task 1. This sample writing task mirrors very closely what you will see on the PARCC. For each task, you will be given two blank pages for prewriting and will type your draft.

You may want to look at the PARCC scoring rubric found in Appendix A before you begin. Try to imitate actual test-taking conditions as closely as possible. Time yourself. Type your response. Try to use the guidelines above to structure your work. When you have finished, use the writer's checklist to ensure that your writing is the very best that it can be.

## Checklist for Narrative Writing

- [ ] Have a strong opening.
- [ ] Introduce a narrator/characters.
- [ ] Sequence events to unfold.
- [ ] Use dialogue and description to develop experiences and events.
- [ ] Use a variety of transitional words and phrases.
- [ ] Use concrete words and phrases and sensory details.
- [ ] Provide a conclusion.

# GUIDED PRACTICE—NARRATIVE WRITING TASK

Read "A Fairy Story." Then write a story based on the prompt that follows. After the question is a sample response that shows one possible example of how the question can be answered. A sample of the prewriting is also included.

### A Fairy Story: An Excerpt from *Rebecca of Sunnybrook Farm*
### by Kate Douglas Wiggins

1   There was once a tired and rather poverty-stricken Princess who dwelled in a cottage on the great highway between two cities. She was not as unhappy as thousands of others; indeed, she had much to be grateful for, but the life she lived and the work she did were hard for one who was so slender.

2   Now the cottage stood by the edge of a great green forest where the wind was always singing in the branches and the sunshine filtering through the leaves.

3   And one day when the Princess was sitting by the wayside quite tired from her labor in the fields, she saw a golden chariot rolling down the King's Highway and in it a person who could be none other than somebody's Fairy Godmother on her way to the Court. The chariot halted at her door, and though the Princess had read of such generous persons, she never dreamed for an instant that one of them could ever alight at her cottage.

4   "If you are tired, poor little Princess, why do you not go into the cool green forest and rest?" asked the Fairy Godmother.

5   "Because I have no time," she answered. "I must go back to my plow."

6   "Is that your plow leaning by the tree, and is it not too heavy?"

7   "It is heavy," answered the Princess, "but I love to turn the hard earth into soft furrows and know that I am making good soil where my seeds may grow. When I feel the weight too much, I try to think of the harvest."

**8**  The golden chariot passed on, and the two talked no more together that day; nevertheless the King's messengers were busy, for they whispered one word into the ear of the Fairy Godmother and another into the ear of the Princess, though so faintly that neither of them realized that the King had spoken.

**9**  The next morning a strong man knocked at the cottage door, and doffing his hat to the Princess said: "A golden chariot passed me yesterday, and one within it flung me a purse of coins, saying: Go out into the King's Highway and search until you find a cottage and a heavy plow leaning against a tree near by. Enter and say to the Princess whom you will find there: "I will guide the plow and you must go and rest, or walk in the cool green forest; for this is the command of your Fairy Godmother."

**10**  And the same thing happened every day, and every day the tired Princess walked in the green wood. Many times she caught the glitter of the chariot and ran into the Highway to give thanks to the Fairy Godmother; but she was never fleet enough to reach the spot. She could only stand with eager eyes and longing heart as the chariot passed by. Yet she never failed to catch a smile, and sometimes a word or two floated back to her, words that sounded like: "I would not be thanked. We are all children of the same King, and I am only his messenger."

**11**  Now as the Princess walked daily in the green forest, hearing the wind singing in the branches and seeing the sunlight filter through the lattice-work of green leaves, there came into her thoughts that had lain asleep in the stifling air of the cottage and the weariness of guiding the plow. And by and by she took a needle from her girdle and pricked the thoughts on the leaves of the trees and sent them into the air to float hither and thither. And it came to pass that people began to pick them up, and holding them against the sun, to read what was written on them, and this was because the simple little words on the leaves were only, after all, a part of one of the

King's messages, such as the Fairy Godmother dropped continually from her golden chariot.

**12** But the miracle of the story lies deeper than all this.

**13** Whenever the Princess pricked the words upon the leaves she added a thought of her Fairy Godmother, and folding it close within, sent the leaf out on the breeze to float hither and thither and fall where it would. And many other little Princesses felt the same impulse and did the same thing. And as nothing is ever lost in the King's Dominion, so these thoughts and wishes and hopes, being full of love and gratitude, had no power to die, but took unto themselves other shapes and lived on forever. They cannot be seen, our vision is too weak; nor heard, our hearing is too dull; but they can sometimes be felt, and we know not what force is stirring our hearts to nobler aims.

## Prose Constructed Response—Narrative Task

In "A Fairy Story," many of the characters complete acts of kindness that help others, and all of the acts are connected. The Princess writes notes on the leaves in the forest, and they are found by the people who live in the Kingdom.

Write a story about a person that found one of the Princess's notes and how it impacted his or her day. Be sure to include details about the story that you read in your response (setting, character traits, etc.).

## Sample Prewriting

| Story Elements | |
| --- | --- |
| Character | Bob the Blacksmith, Driver, horses |
| Setting | A road in the kingdom |
| Problem | Bob has no money to feed his family AND the horse's shoe broke. |
| Solution | Bob fixes the horse's shoe, and the driver gives him two gold coins. |
| Possible title | The Leaf That Said Stop! |

## Sample Response

### The Leaf That Said Stop!

It was a dull and dreary day. Bob the Blacksmith had been walking along the path and feeling quite sad. He had no money to feed his family, and his children were hungry. As he trudged down the road, Bob thought, "What can I do to help my family?" Suddenly, a green leaf floated in front of him.

Bob grabbed the leaf. It was so green compared to all the brown and gray surrounding him. When he looked closely at the leaf he saw the word "stop" written on the leaf. The blacksmith was surprised. What could this mean? Bob stopped in his tracks while he considered this.

As he stood on the road, he suddenly heard a loud clamor behind him. As the blacksmith turned, he saw a golden carriage. One of the horses was limping as the carriage slowly came down the lane. When the carriage stopped in front of him, Bob asked what the problem was. The driver replied, "One of my horses lost his shoe."

The blacksmith said, "I can help you with that." The blacksmith pulled out his tools and fixed the horse's shoe. The driver of the carriage was so happy that he gave the blacksmith two golden coins. The blacksmith was overjoyed. These coins would provide enough food to feed his family for a month. The blacksmith knew that his luck was changing, and all because of the word "stop."

## Evaluation of the Sample Narrative Writing Task

After spending thirty minutes typing your response, you should begin the process of reading through and editing your work.

Spend the first few minutes rereading what you have written to make sure that your ideas make sense.

### Do you have a logical beginning, middle, and end?

The title "The Leaf That Said Stop!" grabs the reader right away. By using an exclamation mark, you let the reader know that something interesting is going to happen in the story. Using a startling fact (a leaf that says "stop"?!?) also helps to draw the reader in. This will make the reader want to read the story to find out what it is about.

The writer introduces the characters and setting in the first paragraph. In addition, the writer explains the problem of the story—Bob needs money to feed his family. Giving the character a name is an effective strategy in narrative writing.

In the middle of the story, the author introduces another element, the leaf. This leaf causes the main character to stop in the middle of the road, which allows the writer to introduce the solution to the problem in the story. The story concludes with a solution to the problem connected to the title of the story.

### Does the piece have a single focus?

The piece is focused. It answers the questions presented in the prompt. There are no extraneous details in the story.

## Did you include a strong opening and closing sentence?

This story includes a strong opening and closing sentence. "*It was a dull and dreary day*" introduces the reader to the tone of the story and provides background for the problem in the story. It also introduces that setting. "*The blacksmith knew that his luck was changing, and all because of the word stop*" is a closing that wraps up the events of the story. It calls attention to the importance of the leaf, and how it helped change the luck of the blacksmith.

## Did you include the important things from your prewriting?

The story closely follows the prewriting outlined by the writer.

In this story, spelling, punctuation, and capitalization are correct. However, it is important for you to reread your own story carefully to check for these errors. They should be corrected to the best of your ability. A final read-through should focus on adding descriptive language to the story. This type of language is used throughout the story to help the reader picture what is happening. Strong verbs (trudged, floated, grabbed) and adjectives (clamor, golden, overjoyed) clearly illustrate the events in the story.

## Writing Rubric

Your writing will be scored using a rubric. The Narrative Writing Rubric is comprised of two parts—written expression and knowledge of language and conventions.

In the sample narrative prompt on page 102, the writer is asked to use details from the story to create a new narrative text. In the sample story, the writer includes details that are aligned with "A Fairy Story." The setting, theme, problem, and solution of "The Leaf That Said Stop!" are congruent with the anchor text. If the writer had set this story in a futuristic city with animals as the main characters, it would not be aligned with the anchor text and task. The writing is well organized and uses language to clarify the ideas presented in the story. The rubric for Written Expression is listed on page 106. This section of the rubric is worth 9 points out of a total of 12 points for the prose constructed-response task.

| Construct Measured | |
|---|---|
| **Written Expression** | |
| **Score Point 3** | The student response:<br><br>—is effectively developed with narrative elements and is consistently appropriate to the task.<br>—is effectively organized with clear and coherent writing.<br>—uses language effectively to clarify ideas. |
| **Score Point 2** | The student response:<br><br>—is developed with some narrative elements and is generally appropriate to the task.<br>—is organized with mostly coherent writing.<br>—uses language that is mostly effective to clarify ideas. |
| **Score Point 1** | The student response:<br><br>—is minimally developed with few narrative elements and is limited in its appropriateness to the task.<br>—demonstrates limited organization and coherence.<br>—uses language to express ideas with limited clarity. |
| **Score Point 0** | The student response:<br><br>—is undeveloped and/or inappropriate to the task.<br>—lacks organization and coherence.<br>—does not use language to express ideas with clarity. |

In Knowledge of Language and Conventions, the writer is asked to use correct grammar, spelling, capitalization, and punctuation. It is important to write well, so that the meaning of your writing is clear. It is important to edit and check for errors during revising and editing time to earn as many points as possible on this section of the rubric (displayed below). This section of the rubric is worth 3 of the 12 points for the prose constructed-response task.

| Construct Measured | |
|---|---|
| **Knowledge of Language and Conventions** | |
| **Score Point 3** | The student response to the prompt: demonstrates full command of the conventions of standard English at an appropriate level of complexity. There may be a few minor errors in mechanics, grammar, and usage, but meaning is clear. |
| **Score Point 2** | The student response to the prompt: demonstrates some command of the conventions of standard English at an appropriate level of complexity. There may be errors in mechanics, grammar, and usage that occasionally impede understanding, but the meaning is generally clear |
| **Score Point 1** | The student response to the prompt: demonstrates limited command of the conventions of standard English at an appropriate level of complexity. There may be errors in mechanics, grammar, and usage that often impede understanding. |
| **Score Point 0** | The student response to the prompt does not: demonstrate command of the conventions of standard English at the appropriate level of complexity. Frequent and varied errors in mechanics, grammar, and usage impede understanding. |

# INDEPENDENT PRACTICE—NARRATIVE WRITING TASK

Read "The Four Brothers." There are two sample prompts following the story that you can use to practice your narrative writing.

### The Four Brothers

### by the Brothers Grimm

1    "Dear children," said a poor man to his four sons, "I have nothing to give you; you must go out into the wide world and try your luck. Begin by learning some craft or another, and see how you can get on." So the four brothers took their walking-sticks in their hands, and their little bundles on their shoulders, and after bidding their father goodbye, went all out at the gate together. When they had got on some way they came to four crossways, each leading to a different country. Then the eldest said, "Here we must part; but this day four years we will come back to this spot, and in the meantime each must try what he can do for himself."

2    So each brother went his way; and as the eldest was hastening on a man met him, and asked him where he was going, and what he wanted. "I am going to try my luck in the world, and should like to begin by learning some art or trade," answered he. "Then," said the man, "go with me, and I will teach you to become the cunningest thief that ever was." "No," said the other, "that is not an honest calling, and what can one look to earn by it in the end but the gallows?" "Oh!" said the man, "you need not fear the gallows; for I will only teach you to steal what will be fair game: I meddle with nothing but what no one else can get or care anything about, and where no one can find you out." So the young man agreed to follow his trade, and he soon showed himself so clever, that nothing could escape him that he had once set his mind upon.

3    The second brother also met a man, who, when he found out what he was setting out upon, asked him what craft he meant to follow. "I do not know yet," said he. "Then come with me, and be

a star-gazer. It is a noble art, for nothing can be hidden from you, when once you understand the stars." The plan pleased him much, and he soon became such a skillful stargazer, that when he had served out his time, and wanted to leave his master, he gave him a glass, and said, "With this you can see all that is passing in the sky and on earth, and nothing can be hidden from you."

4   The third brother met a huntsman, who took him with him, and taught him so well all that belonged to hunting, that he became very clever in the craft of the woods; and when he left his master he gave him a bow, and said, "Whatever you shoot at with this bow you will be sure to hit."

5   The youngest brother likewise met a man who asked him what he wished to do. "Would not you like," said he, "to be a tailor?" "Oh, no!" said the young man; "sitting cross-legged from morning to night, working backwards and forwards with a needle and thread, will never suit me." "Oh!" answered the man, "that is not my sort of tailoring; come with me, and you will learn quite another kind of craft from that." Not knowing what better to do, he came into the plan, and learnt tailoring from the beginning; and when he left his master, he gave him a needle, and said, "You can sew anything with this, be it as soft as an egg or as hard as steel; and the joint will be so fine that no seam will be seen."

6   After the space of four years, at the time agreed upon, the four brothers met at the four cross-roads; and having welcomed each other, set off towards their father's home, where they told him all that had happened to them, and how each had learned some craft.

7   Then, one day, as they were sitting before the house under a very high tree, the father said, "I should like to try what each of you can do in this way." So he looked up, and said to the second son, "At the top of this tree there is a finch's nest; tell me how many eggs there are in it." The star-gazer took his glass, looked up, and said, "Five." "Now," said the father to the eldest son, "take away the

eggs without letting the bird that is sitting upon them and hatching them know anything of what you are doing." So the cunning thief climbed up the tree, and brought away to his father the five eggs from under the bird; and it never saw or felt what he was doing, but kept sitting on at its ease. Then the father took the eggs, and put one on each corner of the table, and the fifth in the middle, and said to the huntsman, "Cut all the eggs in two pieces at one shot." The huntsman took up his bow, and at one shot struck all the five eggs as his father wished.

8   "Now comes your turn," said he to the young tailor; "sew the eggs and the young birds in them together again, so neatly that the shot shall have done them no harm." Then the tailor took his needle, and sewed the eggs as he was told; and when he had done, the thief was sent to take them back to the nest, and put them under the bird without its knowing it. Then she went on sitting, and hatched them: and in a few days they crawled out, and had only a little red streak across their necks, where the tailor had sewn them together.

9   "Well done, sons!" said the old man; "you have made good use of your time, and learnt something worth the knowing; but I am sure I do not know which ought to have the prize. Oh, that a time might soon come for you to turn your skill to some account!" Not long after this there was a great bustle in the country, for the king's daughter had been carried off by a mighty dragon, and the king mourned over his loss day and night, and made it known that whoever brought her back to him should have her for a wife. Then the four brothers said to each other, "Here is a chance for us; let us try what we can do." And they agreed to see whether they could not set the princess free. "I will soon find out where she is, however," said the star-gazer, as he looked through his glass; and he soon cried out, "I see her afar off, sitting upon a rock in the sea, and I can spy the dragon close by, guarding her." Then he went to the king, and asked for a ship for himself and his brothers; and they sailed together over the sea, till they came to the right place. There they

found the princess sitting, as the star-gazer had said, on the rock; and the dragon was lying asleep, with his head upon her lap. "I dare not shoot at him," said the huntsman, "for I should kill the beautiful young lady also." "Then I will try my skill," said the thief, and went and stole her away from under the dragon, so quietly and gently that the beast did not know it, but went on snoring.

**10** Then away they hastened with her full of joy in their boat towards the ship; but soon came the dragon roaring behind them through the air; for he awoke and missed the princess. But when he got over the boat, and wanted to pounce upon them and carry off the princess, the huntsman took up his bow and shot him straight through the heart so that he fell down dead. They were still not safe; for he was such a great beast that in his fall he overset the boat, and they had to swim in the open sea upon a few planks. So the tailor took his needle, and with a few large stitches put some of the planks together; and he sat down upon these, and sailed about and gathered up all pieces of the boat; and then tacked them together so quickly that the boat was soon ready, and they then reached the ship and got home safe.

**11**   When they had brought home the princess to her father, there was great rejoicing; and he said to the four brothers, "One of you shall marry her, but you must settle amongst yourselves which it is to be."' Then there arose a quarrel between them; and the star-gazer said, "If I had not found the princess out, all your skill would have been of no use; therefore she ought to be mine." "Your seeing her would have been of no use," said the thief, "'if I had not taken her away from the dragon; therefore she ought to be mine." "No, she is mine," said the huntsman; "for if I had not killed the dragon, he would, after all, have torn you and the princess into pieces." "And if I had not sewn the boat together again," said the tailor, "you would all have been drowned, therefore she is mine." Then the king put in a word, and said, "Each of you is right; and as all cannot have the young lady, the best way is for neither of you to have her: for the truth is, there is somebody she likes a great deal better. But to make up for your loss, I will give each of you, as a reward for his skill, half a kingdom." So the brothers agreed that this plan would be much better than either quarrelling or marrying a lady who had no mind to have them. And the king then gave to each half a kingdom, as he had said; and they lived very happily the rest of their days, and took good care of their father; and somebody took better care of the young lady, than to let either the dragon or one of the craftsmen have her again.

## Narrative Writing Task 1

The four brothers all have different talents in the story. They use these talents to solve problems in different ways. Think about what you know about the brothers, and write a story about a new problem that they will face. Be sure to include how each brother used his talent to solve the problem.

---

---

---

---

---

---

---

---

---

---

---

---

---

## Narrative Writing Task 2

Each brother met someone different in the story who taught him a skill. Choose one of the brothers to write a story about. Identify the skill that he learned, and write a story that explains how he learned this skill. Use characters and details from "The Four Brothers" in your story.

---

---

---

---

---

---

---

---

---

---

---

---

---

---

## COMMON CORE TIP: NARRATIVE WRITING

**> For Students:** Select a fiction book to read. Read the first section or chapter and then close the book. Try to write a story that continues what you just read. Continue reading and think about how your story compares to that of the author!

**> For Parents:** Sit down with your child and review his or her story. Give your child a star and a wish—a compliment about what he or she wrote and something that you wish had been included in the story.

**> For Teachers:** Writing Standard 4.3 addresses the requirements for narrative writing. Review these requirements (listed below) to ensure that students' writing is structured to meet the grade-level requirements.

- Include an opening that introduces the narrator/characters and establishes a situation.

- Use dialogue and description to tell about the events and characters.

- Use transitions.

- Use phrases and sensory details.

- Provide a conclusion.

# Test-Taking Strategies for Computer-Based Testing

# CHAPTER 6

Taking the PARCC test will have similarities to other tests that you have taken. Something that might be different about the PARCC is that this test is taken on the computer. This chapter will present some general test-taking strategies as well as strategies specific to online testing and the PARCC Assessment.

## General Testing Strategies

- Read the directions carefully and make sure that you understand them.
- Think about the genre, title of the selection, and any pictures or headings you might see. Use this information to make predictions about what you think the passage will be about before you start reading.
- Preview the questions before you start reading the passage.
- Read every possible answer for the multiple-choice questions, and select the choice that *best* answers the question. Eliminate answers that do not make sense.
- Read and respond to items one at a time rather than thinking about the whole test.
- Reread the passage when you are not sure of the answer.
- Complete every question. Even if you don't know the answer, make your best guess using the information that you have.
- Don't spend too much time on any one question. Skip difficult questions and go back to them.
- If you finish the test early, go back and check your answers.
- Keep a good attitude. Think positively!

## Strategies for Online Testing

When you take the PARCC Assessment, you should plan to take the PARCC Tutorial to help you understand all of the features of the TestNav System. The tutorial can be found on the PARCC website. Go to *http://practice.parcc.testnav.com*. Elements of TestNav are explained on page 122.

## Navigating the Test

(Refer to the sample questions on pages 5 and 6)

The toolbar at the top of the screen will help you navigate the test and answer the questions. The following items appear on the toolbar at the top of the screen.

**Left/Right Arrow:** Use the arrows at the top of the screen to move back and forth between the pages of the test.

**Review Button:** Press the review button to see which questions have been answered, not answered, or flagged for review. On this screen, you can easily move between questions that are not answered or flagged by clicking the view button.

**Flag Button:** The flag button allows you to flag a question for further review. You might want to use this button if a question is hard and you want to make sure that you come back to it later in the test.

**Pointer Icon:** The pointer icon is the default tool. This icon will be used to select answers on the test. Be sure the pointer icon is selected whenever you are answering the questions on the test.

**Eliminate Choice Tool:** This tool, displayed as an X in a gray circle, is used to eliminate answer choices on the test. You should use this tool to eliminate answers that you know are not correct. This will place a large red X over these choices. Be sure to switch back to the pointer tool to select the correct answer.

**Exit/Accessibility Icon:** On the right-hand side of the screen, next to your name is a drop down menu that will allow you to exit the test and select additional accessibility options.

**Test Information Bar:** The gray bar below the toolbar displays the section number, test name, question number, and number of items in each section.

**Text Highlighter Tool:** When you are reading the passage, you are able to highlight important ideas and details as you are reading. Use your mouse to highlight the text that you want to remember. When you highlight this text, four boxes will display where you can select the color highlighter that you want to use. As you continue to read on, the highlighting will remain.

**Scrollbar:** The scrollbar will allow you to see all of the information on the page. There are two scrollbars on the page—a passage scrollbar and a page scrollbar.

**Video Player:** If you are asked to watch a video you will be able to play and pause the video. You can watch it as many times as you need. There will be a scrollbar that you can use to move to specific parts of the video. You will also be able to adjust the volume.

## Accessibility Features for All Students

**Magnifier:** If you need to make a text or picture bigger, you can use the magnification tool. This tool looks like a magnifying glass and will increase the size of the image/text in the circle. If you need to increase the size of all of the font on the test, you can press CTRL + to increase the size, and CTRL − to decrease the size. If you are using a touchscreen device, you can use the pinch and zoom motions to increase the font size.

**Line Reader:** The line reader tool can be used to hide the other text or information on the screen. This tool is similar to using a bookmark or a sheet of paper under the lines of text to guide you as you read.

## Additional Accommodations

If you learn differently from other students, you may be able to use additional accommodations on the test. These accommodations are designed to make the test fair and to help you to be successful. You will only be able to use these accommodations if you have an IEP or a 504 plan, or if English is your second language. A complete list of these accommodations are listed in the *PARCC Accessibility Features and Accommodations Manual,* which can be found on the PARCC online website (*www.parcconline.org*). A few additional accommodations are listed below, and you can review the manual for additional accommodations and explanations.

- Change Background/Foreground Color
- Answer Masking
- Text to Speech (for some parts of the test)
- Predictive Spelling
- Extended Time

## The Test-Taking Experience

When you sit down on your first day of the PARCC Assessment you might be wondering what to expect. The next few paragraphs explain how the testing experience works, and provide some tips.

When you sit down at the computer, you will be asked to log into the test. You will be given a username and password to type in. Once you login, the teacher will read directions for the test. Then you will be asked to enter a seal code. The seal code will be written on the board by your teacher. When directed, you will enter the code, and the test will start. Your teacher will keep track of time on the board.

You will wear headphones when taking the test. You will also be given two sheets of scrap paper. Adjust the volume before the test begins.

Be sure that your name is displayed that the top right of the screen. If it is not your name, please let your teacher know right away. Your teacher will go over directions, and then you will begin the test. Above the first passage, there will be some text in bold. This bold text will give you important information about what you will be reading in the selection, and the type of Prose Constructed Response that you will answer. It is important to read this before you read the passage, to help you focus your reading. After reading this bold text, use the arrows at the top of the screen to read the questions in this section. One click of the right arrow will move you to the next question. After you have finished reading all the questions, use the left arrow to go back to the first question, or click the review button to view the first question, and begin reading the passage.

When you are reading the passage, note that there are black circles with numbers in them. This tells you the paragraph number. The paragraph number might be useful when answering questions. If a question refers to line numbers, those will be displayed automatically, instead of paragraph numbers.

You will need to scroll down to read the entire passage. If you are using a mouse, you can use the scroll wheel in the middle of the mouse to do this. If not, you can use your cursor, or finger (for touchscreen devices), to click on the black bar and move up and down the screen. Please note that there are two scrollbars on the screen. The first scrollbar is in the middle of the screen for the passage only. This is called the passage scroll. The second scrollbar is on the right-hand side of the screen and is called the page scroll. This scrollbar will move the entire page up and down, and is often used to display the questions. If you are answering a question that deals with multiple passages, you will be able to view both of them by clicking on the tab at the top of the passage boxes.

While you are reading the passage, you can highlight parts of the text that you think are important. Click and highlight the section of the text that you want to remember. A toolbar will pop up with three different color choices (yellow, pink, and blue) that you can use to take notes. In addition, you can use the white box to un-highlight the text as well.

Many of the questions that you answer will be multiple-choice, and you will have to select the answers to Part A and Part B by clicking in the circles next to each answer choice (you can also click on the answer choice as well to select that answer). Some questions will ask you to select multiple items from a list. These question types are called multiple-select questions. The question stem will indicate that you should select multiple responses or all that apply. You will also know that is a multiple-select question because the circles next to the answer choices will change to squares.

Some technology-enhanced questions will ask you to select, drag, or highlight answer choices. Be sure that you read the directions carefully so that you can understand what you are being asked to do. If you are trying to drag or click something, and it is not working, that may mean that you have too many items selected. For example, if the question asks you to drag three items into box, and you already have three items there, you will not be able to bring any additional items into the box until you remove one.

If you are required to answer a Prose Constructed Response question, you will type your response on the computer. The typing area has some basic word processing features. To help you organize your writing, you can use **bold**, *italic* or <u>underlined</u> font when typing. You can also create bulleted or numbered lists in your writing. The cut feature and copy and paste feature can help you move sentences and paragraphs around during the revision process. Undo and Redo buttons allow you to fix changes that you have made. Please be aware that there is no spell check option in the word processor. Do your best with spelling. Remember, you should use your scrap paper for your prewriting. You will not get credit for any work that you do on your scrap paper.

When you are finished with a section of the test, you will be asked to submit your answers. Do not submit your work until you are sure that you have answered all of the questions to the best of your ability. Once you submit your answers, you will not be able to go back into that section of the test, and you will be done testing for the day.

## Things to Practice Before the Test

Before the test, make sure that you are familiar completing the following tasks on the computer. You might practice some of these tasks at school, but you can also practice them at home. It is important to find out what type of device you will be using for testing and to practice these tasks on that type of device. The test can be taken on a desktop computer, a laptop, or a tablet device (with a touchscreen).

**Scrolling:** Practice scrolling up and down a screen to read a long piece of text. Most web pages use the scroll feature.

**Word Processing:** Use word processing software to practice how to bold, highlight, and underline, as well as copy and paste. Become familiar with the Undo and Redo buttons.

**Composing on the Computer:** In school, most kids write stories/essays on paper. After they are finished revising and editing, they might type them to produce a published copy. Composing on the computer is a slightly different skill. It is important that you practice writing a first draft on the computer so that you can get used to this process. Editing and revising are also different on the computer, so practice using the delete and backspace keys, highlighting and moving text, and using the cursor to move to certain sections of your text.

**Highlight:** Practice using the mouse or touchscreen to highlight and select text.

**Drag/Drop:** Practice clicking and dragging objects around. This can be done with a picture in your word processing software, in games, or by taking the practice PARCC Tests.

**Select:** Practice using the mouse or touchscreen to select answers. Take an online quiz or test to practice this skill.

**Watching Videos:** Watch a video online and practice playing and pausing. Learn to fast forward and rewind by dragging the video scrollbar. Practice finding specific times in the video by using the elapsed time display. Finally, practice adjusting the volume controls so that you can clearly hear the audio.

**Typing:** You must practice typing so that you can quickly and accurately respond to Prose Constructed-Response questions. There are many free online typing programs that will teach you how to type. You can also practice typing by composing stories on the computer, writing emails, or chatting (with your parents' permission!).

# Practice Test 1

## Unit 1

### Literary Analysis Task

Today you will read two folktales: "The Nightingale" and "Old Joe and the Carpenter." After you read the passages and answer the questions, you will write an essay that explains how the characters' actions impact the plot of the story.

### The Nightingale
#### A Chinese Tale

1   Long ago, in the far-off land of China, deep in the forest, there lived a nightingale. The nightingale sang a song so beautiful that the other animals of the forest would stop to listen to her sing.

2   Nightingale: Tra-la-lee! Tra-la-lee! La-la-tra-la-lee!

3   Emperor: Who is that singing? That is the most beautiful singing I have ever heard! Servants come here at once!

4   Servant 1: Yes, mighty emperor?

**5** Servant 2: What can we do for you?

**6** Emperor: Do you hear that singing?

**7** Nightingale: Tra-la-lee! Tra-la-lee!

**8** Servant 1: Yes, it is lovely.

**9** Emperor: Well, I must have it! Please find whoever is singing and bring him or her to me. We will dine together.

**10** So the servants went off to find the singer. They listened to every animal they met. They listened to the cow, "Moo." They listened to the frogs, "Rib-bit." They walked deeper and deeper into the forest until at last they heard," Tra-la-lee! Tra-la-lee!"

**11** Servant 1: There she is, a small gray bird.

**12** Servant 2: I don't believe it. Such beautiful music from such a plain-looking bird.

**13** Servant 1: Miss Nightingale, our emperor loves your singing. He has sent us to invite you for dinner.

**14** Nightingale: It would be a pleasure. Tra-la-lee. Let's go to the palace.

**15** They arrived at the palace. The emperor had a special feast prepared, and many people came to hear the nightingale's song.

**16** Emperor: My dear nightingale, please sing for us.

**17** Nightingale: Tra-la-lee! Tra-la-lee!

**18** The Emperor did enjoy the song. He loved it so much that he decided to keep the nightingale guarded in a beautiful cage. Soon, the nightingale grew homesick. One day, the emperor received a golden toy bird as a present. It was encrusted in diamonds and was the most beautiful thing he had ever seen. It would sing a beautiful song when it was wound up. Everyone was so interested in the toy bird that the nightingale was able to open her cage and fly away.

**19**   Emperor: Don't worry; we have a new bird to sing songs.

**20**   Servant 1: But the toy bird sings the same song.

**21**   After a year, the toy bird broke. The Emperor became very sick in his quiet palace.

**22**   Emperor: I need music to help me feel better. I think I hear music coming from outside.

**23**   Nightingale: Tra-la-lee! Tra-la-lee!

**24**   Emperor: You have returned to sing to me! Nightingale, I have missed you! How can I ever repay you?

**25**   Nightingale: Your smile and good health are payment enough. You can do one more thing for me.

**26**   Emperor: Anything!

**27**   Nightingale: I cannot live in the palace. I need to live in the forest, my home. I will visit you often.

**28**   The Emperor promised, so the nightingale returned nightly to sing to the Emperor. No one ever knew the nightingale was the best medicine.

1. **Part A**

   What lesson do you think the Emperor learned from his experience with the nightingale?

   - ○ A. Never try to keep a bird in a cage.
   - ○ B. Songs will keep you healthy.
   - ○ C. You need to treat someone well if you care for him or her.
   - ○ D. It is better to have a toy bird than a live bird.

   **Part B**

   What detail from the story **best** supports your answer to Part A.

   - ○ A. "One day, the emperor received a golden toy bird as a present." (paragraph 18)
   - ○ B. "I need to live in the forest, my home." (paragraph 27)
   - ○ C. "I need music to help me feel better." (paragraph 22)
   - ○ D. "Your smile and good health are payment enough." (paragraph 25)

2. Choose **five** sentences from the list below and arrange them in the correct order to create a summary for "The Nightingale." Write your selections in the boxes provided.

   | |
   |---|
   | The servants walked and found the bird that was singing. |
   | The toy bird was encrusted in diamonds and sang a song when it was wound up. |
   | The Emperor heard the beautiful singing and asked his servants to find whoever was making the song. |
   | The servants heard many animals' sounds—moo, ribbit, and tra-la-lee! |
   | The nightingale returned to the Emperor, but the Emperor agreed that she could live in the forest. |
   | The nightingale escaped and the Emperor became sad when the toy bird broke, because he had no music to listen to. |
   | The Emperor held a feast and everyone listened to the bird sing. |
   | The bird was so plain to make such beautiful music. |

| | |
|---|---|
| 1 | |
| 2 | |
| 3 | |
| 4 | |
| 5 | |

3. **Part A**

Read the sentence from paragraph 12 of "The Nightingale."

> Such beautiful music from such a plain-looking bird.

What does the sentence show about the nightingale?

- ○ A. She is a bird.
- ○ B. The bird says *tra-la-lee*.
- ○ C. The Emperor likes her singing.
- ○ D. Appearance does not matter.

**Part B**

Which detail from the story shows another example of Part A?

- ○ A. "Such beautiful music from such a plain-looking bird." (paragraph 12)
- ○ B. "It was encrusted in diamonds and was the most beautiful thing he had ever seen." (paragraph 18)
- ○ C. "Don't worry; we have a new bird to sing songs." (paragraph 19)
- ○ D. "No one ever knew the nightingale was the best medicine." (paragraph 28)

4. **Part A**

What is the meaning of the word **homesick** as it is used in paragraph 18 of "The Nightingale"?

- ○ A. lonely
- ○ B. angry
- ○ C. sad
- ○ D. ill

**Part B**

Which detail from the story helps the reader understand the meaning of the word?

- ○ A. "Let's go to the palace." (paragraph 14)
- ○ B. "Long ago, in the far-off land of China, deep in the forest, there lived a nightingale." (paragraph 1)
- ○ C. "The Emperor became very sick in his quiet palace." (paragraph 21)
- ○ D. "I need to live in the forest, my home." (paragraph 27)

## Old Joe and the Carpenter

An American Tale

1   Old Joe lived in the country. His lifelong neighbor was his best friend. Their children were grown and their wives were gone; they had only each other and their farms.

2   One day, they had a serious disagreement over a stray calf. It was found on a neighbor's land and both of them claimed it. The two men were stubborn and would not give in. They went back to their farms and stayed there. Weeks went by without a word between them.

3   Old Joe was feeling poorly when he heard a knock at his front door. At first, he thought it was his neighbor. When he opened the door, he was surprised to see a stranger. The man introduced himself as a "carpenter." He carried a toolbox and had kind eyes.

4   He explained that he was looking for work. Old Joe said he had a job or two for the carpenter. He showed the man his neighbor's house. There was a new creek running between the two pieces of property, freshly dug by Old Joe's neighbor, to separate their property.

5   Old Joe asked the carpenter to build a fence on his property so that he would not have to look at the creek. He helped the carpenter get started and then went to get more supplies for the fence. The carpenter worked without rest and finished the job all by himself.

6   When Old Joe returned and saw what the carpenter had built, he was speechless. The carpenter hadn't built a fence; he had built a bridge. The bridge reached from one side of the creek to the other.

7   Old Joe's neighbor crossed the bridge; he was quick to apologize for their misunderstanding. He told Old Joe that he could have the calf. They shook hands and thanked the carpenter for his work. Both of them suggested he stay and complete other jobs they had for him.

8   The carpenter declined the work and said he had to leave; he had more bridges to build.

5. **Part A**

The last sentence of the tale begins as follows:

> "The carpenter **declined** the work..."

What does the word **declined** mean as it is used in this sentence?

- ○ A.  showed
- ○ B.  expected
- ○ C.  refused
- ○ D.  was grateful for

**Part B**

Which phrase from the story **best** supports the answer to Part A.

- ○ A.  "apologized for their misunderstanding" (paragraph 7)
- ○ B.  "thanked the carpenter" (paragraph 7)
- ○ C.  "complete other jobs" (paragraph 7)
- ○ D.  "he had to leave" (paragraph 8)

6. Select two pieces of evidence that describe the setting in "Old Joe and the Carpenter."

- ☐ A.  "Old Joe lived in the country." (paragraph 1)
- ☐ B.  "One day, they had a serious disagreement over a stray calf." (paragraph 2)
- ☐ C.  "The man introduced himself as a 'carpenter.'" (paragraph 3)
- ☐ D.  "There was a new creek running between the two pieces of property, freshly dug by Old Joe's neighbor, to separate their property." (paragraph 4)
- ☐ E.  "When Old Joe returned and saw what the carpenter had built, he was speechless." (paragraph 6)
- ☐ F.  "The carpenter declined the work and said he had to leave; he had more bridges to build." (paragraph 8)

## 7. Prose Constructed Response—Literary Analysis

Both the Emperor and Joe learn important lessons in the stories. Write an essay that explains how the Emperor's and Joe's actions are important to the plots of the stories. Use what you learned about the characters to support your essay.

-------------------------------------------------------------

-------------------------------------------------------------

-------------------------------------------------------------

-------------------------------------------------------------

-------------------------------------------------------------

-------------------------------------------------------------

-------------------------------------------------------------

-------------------------------------------------------------

-------------------------------------------------------------

-------------------------------------------------------------

-------------------------------------------------------------

-------------------------------------------------------------

-------------------------------------------------------------

-------------------------------------------------------------

-------------------------------------------------------------

-------------------------------------------------------------

Read "The Stone in the Road." Then answer the questions.

## The Stone in the Road
### Adapted Tale

1   This story took place long ago in the kingdom of a very wise king, who was always attempting to teach people good habits. He often tested others to see if they were thoughtful, good people. He believed that people should do less complaining and solve their own problems.

2   One night, while everyone slept, he placed a large stone in the road that led past his palace. He hid at the edge of the road to see what would happen.

3   A short time afterward, a soldier marched casually along the road. The soldier's foot struck the rock, and he sprawled in the road. The soldier rose angrily, waving his sword at the rock. He complained to himself as he continued down the road, blaming lazy people for leaving the rock in the road; never once did the soldier think that he should move the stone himself.

4   After a few more minutes, a farmer guided his grain wagon around the rock in the road. He was on his way to the mill to have his grain ground to flour, and he did not have time to stop and remove the rock. "The world is filled with careless, lazy people!" the farmer complained. "Someone should remove the rock from the road so that it doesn't cause an accident."

5   All day long the king secretly watched people go around the rock and complain about lazy people leaving the rock in the road: yet no one touched the rock to move it.

6   It was almost evening when a young girl walked past the palace. She was very tired from working at the mill all day. She spotted the rock and thought, "I should move this rock from the road; it is almost dark and someone may trip and get hurt."

**7**   She struggled with the heavy rock and managed to move it aside. Beneath the rock was a box. She lifted the heavy box out of the hole it was in. On it was written, "This box belongs to the thoughtful one who moves the stone out of the way for others."

**8**   The girl opened the box and discovered it was filled with gold. The news of her find spread throughout the area. The soldier and the farmer and the other passersby went back to the spot in the road to search in the dust for a piece of gold.

**9**   The king announced the find: "As we go through life, we often are faced with obstacles and problems. We may complain while we just walk around them waiting for someone else to solve them, or we can take the time to solve the problems ourselves. If we leave problems for someone else to solve, we are usually disappointed."

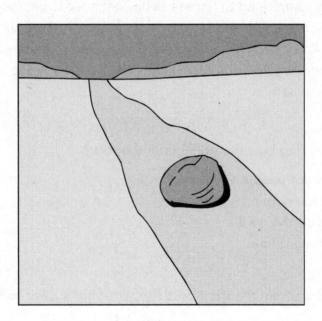

8. **Part A**

Read the following sentence from paragraph 3 of "The Stone in the Road."

> The soldier's foot struck the rock, and he **sprawled** in the road.

What does the word **sprawled** mean as it is used in this sentence?

- ○ A. tripped on a rock
- ○ B. laid on the ground with his arms and legs spread out
- ○ C. crawled on all fours
- ○ D. yelled angrily

**Part B**

What evidence from the story **best** supports your answer to Part A?

- ○ A. "The soldier rose angrily, waving his sword at the rock." (paragraph 3)
- ○ B. "A short time afterward, a soldier marched casually along the road." (paragraph 3)
- ○ C. "He complained to himself as he continued down the road, blaming lazy people for leaving the rock in the road; never once did the soldier think that he should move the stone himself." (paragraph 3)
- ○ D. "She struggled with the heavy rock and managed to move it aside." (paragraph 7)

9. **Part A**

Why did the king bury the gold under the rock?

- ○ A. to teach people a lesson
- ○ B. to hide it from people
- ○ C. to save the gold
- ○ D. to keep it safe

**Part B**

What evidence from the story **best** supports your answer to Part A?

- ○ A. "All day long the king secretly watched people go around the rock and complain about lazy people leaving the rock in the road: yet no one touched the rock to move it." (paragraph 5)
- ○ B. "The girl opened the box and discovered it was filled with gold." (paragraph 8)
- ○ C. "This story took place long ago in the kingdom of a very wise king, who was always attempting to teach people good habits." (paragraph 1)
- ○ D. "One night, while everyone slept, he placed a large stone in the road that led past his palace." (paragraph 2)

10. **Part A**

What is this story mostly about?

- ○ A. lazy people
- ○ B. a box of gold
- ○ C. a stone in the road
- ○ D. a lesson

**Part B**

What detail from the story **best** supports your answer to Part A?

- ○ A. "One night, while everyone slept, he placed a large stone in the road that led past his palace." (paragraph 2)
- ○ B. "If we leave problems for someone else to solve, we are usually disappointed." (paragraph 9)
- ○ C. "All day long the king secretly watched people go around the rock and complain about lazy people leaving the rock in the road: yet no one touched the rock to move it." (paragraph 5)
- ○ D. "The girl opened the box and discovered it was filled with gold." (paragraph 8)

11. Based on the story, what three character traits **best** describe the king? Select the three best traits.

- ☐ A. Wise
- ☐ B. Tricky
- ☐ C. Selfish
- ☐ D. Mean
- ☐ E. Thoughtful
- ☐ F. Observant
- ☐ G. Generous

12. Each of the characters has a different response to the stone in the road. Write a sentence from the list below in the box next to each character's name to show how that character reacted to the stone in the road.

- Moved the cart around the stone
- Tripped over the stone
- Watched the people go by
- Moved the rock to the side
- Made an announcement

| Character | Response to the Stone in the Road |
|---|---|
| Soldier | |
| Farmer | |
| Young Girl | |

13. Select a phrase from the list below that best describes the setting and write it in the middle of the web. Select three sentences from the story that describe the setting and write them in the circles on the outside of the web.

Possible Settings

The palace

A road

The mill

**Sentences**

- "This story took place long ago in the kingdom of a very wise king, who was always attempting to teach people good habits." (paragraph 1)

- "The king announced the find: 'As we go through life, we often are faced with obstacles and problems. We may complain while we just walk around them waiting for someone else to solve them, or we can take the time to solve the problems ourselves. If we leave problems for someone else to solve, we are usually disappointed.'" (paragraph 9)

- "One night, while everyone slept, he placed a large stone in the road that led past his palace." (paragraph 2)

- "She struggled with the heavy rock and managed to move it aside." (paragraph 7)

- "She was very tired from working at the mill all day." (paragraph 6)

- "The soldier and the farmer and the other passersby went back to the spot in the road to search in the dust for a piece of gold." (paragraph 8)

- "'Someone should remove the rock from the road so that it doesn't cause an accident.'" (paragraph 4)

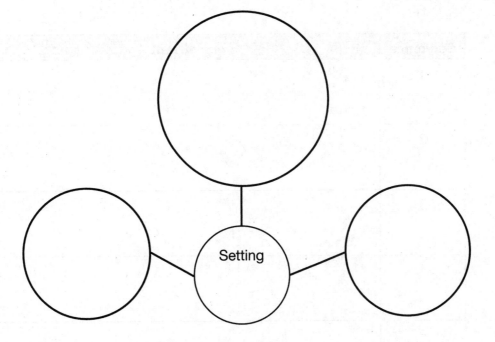

**14.** Write five sentences from the list below, in the correct order, in the boxes to summarize the story.

- "This story took place long ago in the kingdom of a very wise king, who was always attempting to teach people good habits."
- "She struggled with the heavy rock and managed to move it aside."
- "'The world is filled with careless, lazy people!' the farmer complained."
- "On it was written, 'This box belongs to the thoughtful one who moves the stone out of the way for others.'"
- "One night, while everyone slept, he placed a large stone in the road that led past his palace. He hid at the edge of the road to see what would happen."
- "All day long the king secretly watched people go around the rock and complain about lazy people leaving the rock in the road: yet no one touched the rock to move it."
- "She spotted the rock and thought, 'I should move this rock from the road; it is almost dark and someone may trip and get hurt.'"
- "She was very tired from working at the mill all day."

| Sequence | Event |
|---|---|
| 1 | |
| 2 | |
| 3 | |
| 4 | |
| 5 | |

# Unit 2

## Research Simulation Task

Today you will read three texts about symbols in America.

- America's Doorway
- A Proud Lady in the Harbor
- An American Symbol

After you read the passages and answer the questions, you will write an essay that describes the symbols and makes an argument for the symbol that is most important to the heritage of the United States.

### America's Doorway

**1**  On January 1, 1892, the door to America swung open. From then until 1954, more than 12 million immigrants passed through it.

**2**  That doorway was Ellis Island in New York Harbor. It is close to the Statue of Liberty. Seventy percent of all immigrants at the time were processed there. The ancestors of more than 40 percent of Americans arrived here by way of Ellis Island.

**3**  The process for entering the United States was partly based on status. Passengers who could afford to travel with first- and second-class tickets were not considered to be a risk. When the ships docked at piers on the Hudson River, the first- and second-class passengers could leave and pass through Customs. Then they were free to enter the United States.

**4**  The situation was very different for "steerage" or third-class passengers. They traveled to America in crowded and unsanitary conditions. They slept near the bottom of their ships. After the ships docked, they were transported to Ellis Island, where everyone would undergo a medical and legal inspection.

**5**  First they had to pass a physical examination. Some with health problems or diseases such as measles were sent home. About 2 percent were sent back. Others were held in the island's hospital facilities for long periods of time. They were asked questions including name, occupation, and the amount of money they carried with them. Criminals and other risky people were also sent back.

**6** The Ellis Island inspection process would last approximately three to five hours. The inspections took place in the Registry Room (or Great Hall). Doctors would briefly scan every immigrant for obvious physical ailments. This happened very quickly. A doctor could identify numerous medical conditions just by glancing at an immigrant. These were called "six-second physicals." If they were healthy, their papers were checked. If they were in order, people were then allowed to leave. They were now in America.

**7** Eventually, immigration into America slowed down. By 1954, Ellis Island was no longer needed as a processing center.

**8** In 1965, President Lyndon Johnson declared Ellis Island part of the Statue of Liberty National Monument. From 1976 to 1984 the main building was open to the public. Starting in 1984, Ellis Island underwent a major restoration. The $160 million project was the largest historic restoration in U.S. history. The money was raised by donations made by the American people. Now, every year nearly 2 million people visit this important historical site.

1. **Part A**

What does the word **immigrants** mean, as it is used in the article "America's Doorway"?

○ A. wealthy travelers by ship
○ B. people entering a country
○ C. people leaving a country
○ D. someone with no home

**Part B**

Which statement from the article "America's Doorway" **best** supports the answer to Part A?

○ A. "The ancestors of more than 40 percent of Americans arrived here by way of Ellis Island." (paragraph 2)
○ B. "The situation was very different for 'steerage' or third-class passengers." (paragraph 4)
○ C. "First they had to pass a physical examination." (paragraph 5)
○ D. "By 1954, Ellis Island was no longer needed as a processing center." (paragraph 7)

2. **Part A**

Read the sentence below from paragraph 3 of "America's Doorway."

"The process for entering the United States was partly based on status."

Which statement provides the **best** explanation for this sentence?

○ A. Everyone had to go through a long inspection process at Ellis Island.
○ B. First- and second-class passengers were allowed into the United States, while the third-class passengers were sent home.
○ C. First- and second-class passengers were able to enter the United States quickly, but steerage passengers had to undergo a long inspection process at Ellis Island.
○ D. When immigration slowed down, Ellis Island was closed because it was no longer needed.

**Part B:** Which sentence from "America's Doorway" best supports your answer to Part A?

- ○ A. "Then they were free to enter the United States." (paragraph 3)
- ○ B. "After the ships docked, they were transported to Ellis Island, where everyone would undergo a medical and legal inspection." (paragraph 4)
- ○ C. "Eventually, immigration into America slowed down." (paragraph 7)
- ○ D. "Doctors would briefly scan every immigrant for obvious physical ailments." (paragraph 6)

3. Select two problems and two solutions from the list below. Write them in the chart on the next page.

| Problems |
| --- |
| "On January 1, 1892, the door to America swung open." (paragraph 1) |
| "They traveled to America in crowded and unsanitary conditions." (paragraph 4) |
| "Doctors would briefly scan every immigrant for obvious physical ailments." (paragraph 6) |
| "The inspections took place in the Registry Room (or Great Hall)." (paragraph 6) |

| Solutions |
| --- |
| "After the ships docked, they were transported to Ellis Island, where everyone would undergo a medical and legal inspection." (paragraph 4) |
| "The money was raised by donations made by the American people." (paragraph 8) |
| "About 2 percent were sent back. Others were held in the island's hospital facilities for long periods of time." (paragraph 5) |
| "It is close to the Statue of Liberty." (paragraph 2) |

| Problem | Solution |
|---|---|
|  |  |
|  |  |

### A Proud Lady in the Harbor

1   Who wears a crown with seven huge spikes, has an index finger longer than the height of a very tall basketball player, and wears a size 879 in women's shoes? The answer, of course, is the world famous Statue of Liberty. It was the first site that immigrants saw when they arrived in America.

2   In 1884 France gave the Statue to the United States as a symbol of the friendship these two countries had made during the American Revolution. The huge copper structure was shipped to the United States in 1885 in 214 cases. Over the years, the monument has also come to symbolize freedom under America's free form of government.

3   The Statue, whose proper name is "Liberty Enlightening the World," stands proudly 115 feet above New York Harbor. It is a tremendous sculpture of a lady, who is dressed in a loose robe. She holds a torch in her right hand, which is raised high in the air. Her left arm holds a tablet containing the date of the Declaration

of Independence: July 4th, 1776. People hardly notice the broken shackles underfoot, which represent Liberty destroying the chains of slavery. The seven spikes in her crown stand for either the seven seas or the seven continents.

**4** Millions of people visit the Statue annually. Many visitors climb 354 steps to reach the crown, which contains 25 windows. The normal waiting time to climb to the crown in the summer is three hours. Some visitors take an elevator to the base of the statue, where there is an observation balcony and view of the city. The original torch, which was replaced when the structure was restored in the 1980s, is now at the base.

**5** Today, next to the flag of the United States, the Statue is America's most common symbol for freedom.

4. **Part A**

Read the following sentence from paragraph 2 of "A Proud Lady in the Harbor."

> Over the years, the monument has also come to **symbolize freedom** under America's free form of government.

What does the phrase **symbolize freedom** mean as it is used in the sentence?

- ○ A. a picture of a statue
- ○ B. a country where people can make their own choices
- ○ C. the Statue of Liberty
- ○ D. a gift from France

**Part B**

Which sentence from the story **best** supports your answer to Part A?

- ○ A. "The answer, of course, is the world famous Statue of Liberty." (paragraph 1)
- ○ B. "In 1884 France gave the Statue to the United States as a symbol of the friendship these two countries had made during the American Revolution." (paragraph 2)
- ○ C. "The Statue, whose proper name is 'Liberty Enlightening the World,' stands proudly 115 feet above New York Harbor." (paragraph 3)
- ○ D. "Today, next to the flag of the United States, the Statue is America's most common symbol for freedom." (paragraph 5)

**5. Part A**

What is the main idea of the article "A Proud Lady in the Harbor"?

- ○ A. Lady Liberty has a large foot and index finger.
- ○ B. Visitors can either climb many stairs or take the elevator to view different parts of the monument.
- ○ C. The Statue of Liberty is a well-known monument and symbol for freedom.
- ○ D. Visitors to the Statue of Liberty should take more time and notice the important broken shackles by her feet.

**Part B**

Select two details below that **best** support the answer to Part A.

- ☐ A. "The huge copper structure was shipped to the United States in 1885 in 214 cases." (paragraph 2)
- ☐ B. "Many visitors climb 354 steps to reach the crown, which contains 25 windows." (paragraph 4)
- ☐ C. "Over the years, the monument has also come to symbolize freedom under America's free form of government." (paragraph 2)
- ☐ D. "It was the first site that immigrants saw when they arrived in America." (paragraph 1)
- ☐ E. "The Statue, whose proper name is 'Liberty Enlightening the World,' stands proudly 115 feet above New York Harbor." (paragraph 3)
- ☐ F. "The seven spikes in her crown stand for either the seven seas or the seven continents." (paragraph 3)

6. **Part A**

How does the author mainly organize the information in "A Proud Lady in the Harbor"?

○ A.  By stating a problem and how it can be solved
○ B.  By stating a point of view and then comparing ideas
○ C.  By explaining causes and effects of an event
○ D.  By explaining the events in the order that they happened

**Part B**

Which sentence from the article **best** supports the structure in the answer to Part A?

○ A.  "Who wears a crown with seven huge spikes, has an index finger longer than the height of a very tall basketball player, and wears a size 879 in women's shoes?" (paragraph 1)
○ B.  "The Statue, whose proper name is 'Liberty Enlightening the World,' stands proudly 115 feet above New York Harbor." (paragraph 3)
○ C.  "Many visitors climb 354 steps to reach the crown, which contains 25 windows." (paragraph 4)
○ D.  "In 1884 France gave the Statue to the United States as a symbol of the friendship these two countries had made during the American Revolution." (paragraph 2)

## An American Symbol

The American Bald Eagle celebrated and grand,

In 1782, became the symbol of a new land.

Found from Alaska to the Florida Coast;

**Line** It seemed like the perfect national bird to most.

**(5)** Ben Franklin argued the Eagle's character was lacking;

Thus, another native bird, the turkey, received his backing.

After years of debate the Bald Eagle was crowned;

Its majestic images are now world renowned.

Flying to speeds of 100 miles per hour and hunting with keen
**(10)** eyesight,

Eagles leave their diet of fish and other small prey less than a fair
fight.

Bald eagles build enormous 2000-pound nests,

A lofty home for 20 to 30 years, whenever they need to rest.

**(15)** Once an endangered species, the population continues to gain.

Now protected and respected many of them remain.

The Bald Eagle exhibits beauty and proud independence,

The living symbol of America's freedom, spirit, and pursuit of
excellence.

**7. Part A**

Read the sentence from line 6 of the poem, "An American Symbol."

> Thus, another **native** bird, the turkey, received his backing.

What does the word **native** mean as it is used in this sentence?

- ○ A. a symbol of our country
- ○ B. found in America
- ○ C. endangered
- ○ D. trustworthy

**Part B**

Which line from the poem **best** supports your answer to Part A?

- ○ A. "Its majestic images are now world renowned." (line 8)
- ○ B. "Now protected and respected many of them remain." (line 16)
- ○ C. "Ben Franklin argued the Eagle's character was lacking;" (line 5)
- ○ D. "Found from Alaska to the Florida Coast;" (line 3)

**8. Part A**

Based on information from the poem, "An American Symbol," why was the Bald Eagle selected to become a symbol of our country?

- ○ A. Ben Franklin thought the Eagle would be a good choice.
- ○ B. The Bald Eagle is found in many states and symbolizes beauty and independence.
- ○ C. The Bald Eagle was an endangered species, but now it is protected.
- ○ D. The bird flies at speeds of 100 miles per hour and makes large nests.

**Part B**

What line from the poem **best** supports your answer to Part A?

- ○ A. "Ben Franklin argued the Eagle's character was lacking;" (line 5)
- ○ B. "It seemed like the perfect national bird to most." (line 4)
- ○ C. "Now protected and respected many of them remain." (line 16)
- ○ D. "Found from Alaska to the Florida Coast;" (line 3)

## 9. Prose Constructed Response—Research Simulation Task

You have read three texts about important symbols to our country.

- "America's Doorway"
- "A Proud Lady in the Harbor"
- "An American Symbol"

Identify the three symbols discussed in the three texts and provide information about the symbols. Then select the one of the three symbols that you think is the most important symbol to the heritage of the United States, and explain why. Be sure to use details and examples from the texts to support your argument.

--------------------------------------------------------------------

--------------------------------------------------------------------

--------------------------------------------------------------------

--------------------------------------------------------------------

--------------------------------------------------------------------

--------------------------------------------------------------------

--------------------------------------------------------------------

--------------------------------------------------------------------

--------------------------------------------------------------------

--------------------------------------------------------------------

# Unit 3

## Narrative Writing Task

### A Fairy Story: An Excerpt from *Rebecca of Sunnybrook Farm*
### by Kate Douglas Wiggins

1 There was once a tired and rather poverty-stricken Princess who dwelled in a cottage on the great highway between two cities. She was not as unhappy as thousands of others; indeed, she had much to be grateful for, but the life she lived and the work she did were hard for one who was so slender.

2 Now the cottage stood by the edge of a great green forest where the wind was always singing in the branches and the sunshine filtering through the leaves.

3 And one day when the Princess was sitting by the wayside quite tired from her labor in the fields, she saw a golden chariot rolling down the King's Highway and in it a person who could be none other than somebody's Fairy Godmother on her way to the Court. The chariot halted at her door, and though the Princess had read of such generous persons, she never dreamed for an instant that one of them could ever alight at her cottage.

4 "If you are tired, poor little Princess, why do you not go into the cool green forest and rest?" asked the Fairy Godmother.

5 "Because I have no time," she answered. "I must go back to my plow."

6 "Is that your plow leaning by the tree, and is it not too heavy?"

7 "It is heavy," answered the Princess, "but I love to turn the hard earth into soft furrows and know that I am making good soil where my seeds may grow. When I feel the weight too much, I try to think of the harvest."

**8**   The golden chariot passed on, and the two talked no more together that day; nevertheless the King's messengers were busy, for they whispered one word into the ear of the Fairy Godmother and another into the ear of the Princess, though so faintly that neither of them realized that the King had spoken.

**9**   The next morning a strong man knocked at the cottage door, and doffing his hat to the Princess said: "A golden chariot passed me yesterday, and one within it flung me a purse of coins, saying: Go out into the King's Highway and search until you find a cottage and a heavy plow leaning against a tree nearby. Enter and say to the Princess whom you will find there: "I will guide the plow and you must go and rest, or walk in the cool green forest; for this is the command of your Fairy Godmother."

**10**   And the same thing happened every day, and every day the tired Princess walked in the green wood. Many times she caught the glitter of the chariot and ran into the Highway to give thanks to the Fairy Godmother; but she was never fleet enough to reach the spot. She could only stand with eager eyes and longing heart as the chariot passed by. Yet she never failed to catch a smile, and sometimes a word or two floated back to her, words that sounded like: "I would not be thanked. We are all children of the same King, and I am only his messenger."

**11**   Now as the Princess walked daily in the green forest, hearing the wind singing in the branches and seeing the sunlight filter through the lattice-work of green leaves, there came into her thoughts that had lain asleep in the stifling air of the cottage and the weariness of guiding the plow. And by and by she took a needle from her girdle and pricked the thoughts on the leaves of the trees and sent them into the air to float hither and thither. And it came to pass that people began to pick them up, and holding them against the sun, to read what was written on them, and this was because the simple little words on the leaves were only, after all, a part of one of the King's messages, such as the Fairy Godmother dropped continually from her golden chariot.

**12**  But the miracle of the story lies deeper than all this. Whenever the Princess pricked the words upon the leaves she added a thought of her Fairy Godmother, and folding it close within, sent the leaf out on the breeze to float hither and thither and fall where it would. And many other little Princesses felt the same impulse and did the same thing. And as nothing is ever lost in the King's Dominion, so these thoughts and wishes and hopes, being full of love and gratitude, had no power to die, but took unto themselves other shapes and lived on forever. They cannot be seen, our vision is too weak; nor heard, our hearing is too dull; but they can sometimes be felt, and we know not what force is stirring our hearts to nobler aims.

**13**  The end of the story is not come, but it may be that some day when the Fairy Godmother has a message to deliver in person straight to the King, he will say: "Your face I know; your voice, your thoughts, and your heart. I have heard the rumble of your chariot wheels on the great Highway, and I knew that you were on the King's business. Here in my hand is a sheaf of messages from every quarter of my kingdom. They were delivered by weary and footsore travelers, who said that they could never have reached the gate in safety had it not been for your help and inspiration. Read them, that you may know when and where and how you sped the King's service."

**14**  And when the Fairy Godmother reads them, it may be that sweet odors will rise from the pages, and half-forgotten memories will stir the air; but in the gladness of the moment nothing will be half so lovely as the voice of the King when he said: "Read, and know how you sped the King's service."

1. **Part A**

Which paragraph in the story **best** describes the setting of "A Fairy Story"?

- ○ A. Paragraph 2
- ○ B. Paragraph 4
- ○ C. Paragraph 7
- ○ D. Paragraph 9

**Part B**

Which evidence from the story provides additional details about the setting?

- ○ A. "I have heard the rumble of your chariot wheels on the great Highway, and I knew that you were on the King's business." (paragraph 13)
- ○ B. "Now as the Princess walked daily in the green forest, hearing the wind singing in the branches and seeing the sunlight filter through the lattice-work of green leaves, there came into her thoughts that had lain asleep in the stifling air of the cottage and the weariness of guiding the plow." (paragraph 11)
- ○ C. "And one day when the Princess was sitting by the wayside quite tired from her labor in the fields, she saw a golden chariot rolling down the King's Highway and in it a person who could be none other than somebody's Fairy Godmother on her way to the Court." (paragraph 3)
- ○ D. "Many times she caught the glitter of the chariot and ran into the Highway to give thanks to the Fairy Godmother; but she was never fleet enough to reach the spot." (paragraph 10)

2. **Part A**

Which **best** describes why the Fairy Godmother says that the Princess should take a walk in the woods?

- ○ A. It is hot and sunny out.
- ○ B. The Princess was tired from working in the field all day.
- ○ C. She wanted the Princess to write messages in the leaves.
- ○ D. She wanted to make the King happy.

**Part B**

Which paragraph **best** supports the answer to Part A?

- ○ A. Paragraph 2
- ○ B. Paragraph 3
- ○ C. Paragraph 11
- ○ D. Paragraph 13

3. **Part A**

How does the Princess feel at the end of the story?

- ○ A. thankful
- ○ B. bored
- ○ C. special
- ○ D. tired

**Part B**

What detail **best** supports the answer to Part A?

- ○ A. There was once a tired and rather poverty-stricken Princess who dwelled in a cottage on the great highway between two cities. (paragraph 1)
- ○ B. "'Because I have no time,' she answered. 'I must go back to my plow.'" (paragraph 5)
- ○ C. Many times she caught the glitter of the chariot and ran into the Highway to give thanks to the Fairy Godmother; but she was never fleet enough to reach the spot. (paragraph 10)
- ○ D. But the miracle of the story lies deeper than all this. (paragraph 12)

4. **Part A**

Which character trait **best** describes the Princess in the story?

- ○ A. devious
- ○ B. trustworthy
- ○ C. hardworking
- ○ D. greedy

**Part B**

Select two details below that provide evidence for your answer to Part A.

- ☐ A. "She was not as unhappy as thousands of others; indeed, she had much to be grateful for, but the life she lived and the work she did were hard for one who was so slender." (paragraph 1)
- ☐ B. "The chariot halted at her door, and though the Princess had read of such generous persons, she never dreamed for an instant that one of them could ever alight at her cottage." (paragraph 3)
- ☐ C. "When I feel the weight too much, I try to think of the harvest." (paragraph 7)
- ☐ D. "'I will guide the plow and you must go and rest, or walk in the cool green forest; for this is the command of your Fairy Godmother.'" (paragraph 9)
- ☐ E. "Now as the Princess walked daily in the green forest, hearing the wind singing in the branches and seeing the sunlight filter through the lattice-work of green leaves, there came into her thoughts that had lain asleep in the stifling air of the cottage and the weariness of guiding the plow." (paragraph 11)
- ☐ F. "Here in my hand is a sheaf of messages from every quarter of my kingdom." (paragraph 13)
- ☐ G. "'A golden chariot passed me yesterday, and one within it flung me a purse of coins, saying: Go out into the King's Highway and search until you find a cottage and a heavy plow leaning against a tree nearby.'" (paragraph 9)

**5.** Imagine what the story would be like from the Fairy Godmother's point of view. Consider how it would be different from the story that you read. Rewrite the story to tell it from the Fairy Godmother's point of view.

-------------------------------------------------------------

-------------------------------------------------------------

-------------------------------------------------------------

-------------------------------------------------------------

-------------------------------------------------------------

-------------------------------------------------------------

-------------------------------------------------------------

-------------------------------------------------------------

-------------------------------------------------------------

-------------------------------------------------------------

-------------------------------------------------------------

-------------------------------------------------------------

-------------------------------------------------------------

Read "Chomp! Meat-Eating Plants." Then answer the questions.

## Chomp! Meat-Eating Plants
by Catherine Clarke Fox

**1**   "I want people to get passionate about plants," says Lisa Van Cleef about a new exhibit at the San Francisco Conservatory of Flowers. "Everybody gets excited about the zoo and animals, but once you start looking at plants, you find they have a lot going on, too!"

**2**   Especially the carnivores, or meat eaters, that use the sneakiest of tricks to trap their insect dinners. Take bladderworts, for example. They appear so small and delicate growing in a quiet pond. But these are the fastest-known killers of the plant kingdom, able to suck in unsuspecting mosquito larvae in 1/50 of a second using a trap door!

**3**   Once the trap door closes on the victim, digestive enzymes similar to those in the human stomach slowly consume the insect. When dinner is over, the plant ejects the remains and is ready to trap again.

**4**   Carnivorous plants grow in places with soil that doesn't offer much food value. "You and I could take a vitamin pill," says Van Cleef. "But these amazing plants have had to evolve over thousands of years, developing insect traps to get their nutritional needs met. Just look at all they've done in the fight to survive."

**5**   The traps can be well-disguised to fool the eye, like pitcher plants, which get their name because they look like beautiful pitchers full of nectar.

**6**   The Asian pitcher plant, for example, has a brightly colored rim and an enticing half-closed lid. Curious insects are tempted to come close and take a sip, then slide down the slippery slope to their deaths.

**7** Hair-like growths along the pitcher walls ensure that nothing can scramble out, and the digestive enzymes can get to work. A tiny insect called a midge might be digested in a few hours, but a fly takes a couple of days.

**8** Some of these pitchers are large enough to hold two gallons (7.5 liters). Carnivorous plants only eat people in science fiction movies, but once in a while a small lizard, rodent, or bird will discover that a pitcher plant isn't a good place to get a drink.

**9** Other plants have found different ways to grab a bite. Sundews and butterworts snag snacks with flypaper-like stickiness, while the Venus flytrap snaps shut on its victims.

**10** Carnivorous plants grow mostly in wet areas, from sea level to the mountains. They may seem exotic, but if you live in the United States, you don't have to travel to faraway lands to see some. North America has more carnivorous plant genera than any other continent.

**11** If you can't travel to the exhibit in San Francisco, check out a carnivorous plant guidebook from your local library, and you may discover some growing in your neck of the woods!

---

**Fast Facts**

- The cobra lily (Darlingtonia) has clear cells on top of its pitcher-like trap that work like a skylight. Think about it: Would you rather enter a dark cave, or a light one?
- Some pitcher plants (Nepenthes) trap frogs, and when the frogs are digested, all that remains are little matching frog slippers since the skin on frogs' feet resists digestion.
- Most Nepenthes have two kinds of pitchers, some low to the ground to attract crawling insects, and some higher up to catch those that fly.

6. **Part A**

What is a carnivore?

- ○ A. a plant eater
- ○ B. a meat eater
- ○ C. an insect eater
- ○ D. an animal

**Part B**

What detail from the text **best** supports the definition of the word in Part A?

- ○ A. "Once the trap door closes on the victim, digestive enzymes similar to those in the human stomach slowly consume the insect." (paragraph 3)
- ○ B. "The traps can be well-disguised to fool the eye, like pitcher plants, which get their name because they look like beautiful pitchers full of nectar." (paragraph 5)
- ○ C. "Some of these pitchers are large enough to hold two gallons (7.5 liters)." (paragraph 8)
- ○ D. "Other plants have found different ways to grab a bite." (paragraph 9)

7. **Part A**

What is the main idea of the text?

- ○ A. "Carnivorous plants grow in places with soil that doesn't offer much food value. (paragraph 4)
- ○ B. " Especially the carnivores, or meat eaters, that use the sneakiest of tricks to trap their insect dinners. (paragraph 2)
- ○ C. " A tiny insect called a midge might be digested in a few hours, but a fly takes a couple of days. (paragraph 7)
- ○ D. "Carnivorous plants grow mostly in wet areas, from sea level to the mountains. (paragraph 10)

**Part B**

Select a detail that **best** supports the main idea in Part A?

- ○ A. "They may seem exotic, but if you live in the United States, you don't have to travel to faraway lands to see some." (paragraph 10)
- ○ B. "'You and I could take a vitamin pill,'" says Van Cleef." (paragraph 4)
- ○ C. "Sundews and butterworts snag snacks with flypaper-like stickiness, while the Venus flytrap snaps shut on its victims." (paragraph 9)
- ○ D. "'I want people to get passionate about plants,'" says Lisa Van Cleef about a new exhibit at the San Francisco Conservatory of Flowers." (paragraph 1)

**8. Part A**

Why does the author describe the bladderwort as being sneaky?

- ○ A. It appears to be small and delicate.
- ○ B. It has a slippery slope.
- ○ C. It is brightly colored.
- ○ D. It has a sticky surface.

**Part B**

What is another detail that gives information about the bladderwort?

- ○ A. It eats mosquito eggs.
- ○ B. It has a bowl full of nectar.
- ○ C. It eats frogs.
- ○ D. It has hair to keep insects from escaping.

**9. Part A**

How does the author organize the information in the text?

- ○ A. By stating a problem and how it can be solved
- ○ B. By stating a point of view and then comparing ideas
- ○ C. By explaining the causes and effects of an event
- ○ D. By explaining the events in the order they happened

### Part B

What sentence from the article **best** supports your answer in Part A?

- ○ A. "If you can't travel to the exhibit in San Francisco, check out a carnivorous plant guidebook from your local library, and you may discover some growing in your neck of the woods!" (paragraph 11)
- ○ B. "'But these amazing plants have had to evolve over thousands of years, developing insect traps to get their nutritional needs met. Just look at all they've done in the fight to survive.'" (paragraph 4)
- ○ C. "They may seem exotic, but if you live in the United States, you don't have to travel to faraway lands to see some." (paragraph 10)
- ○ D. "A tiny insect called a midge might be digested in a few hours, but a fly takes a couple of days." (paragraph 7)

## 10. Part A

What is the problem that is presented in this article?

- ○ A. The insects can't escape from the plant.
- ○ B. The pitcher plant has a sweet nectar that attracts bugs.
- ○ C. The pitcher plant cannot digest a frog's feet.
- ○ D. The plants needed to get nutrition in other ways.

### Part B

What sentence from the article **best** shows a solution to the problem selected in Part A.

- ○ A. "Some pitcher plants (Nepethenes) trap frogs, and when the frogs are digested, all that remains are little matching frog slippers since the skin on frogs' feet resists digestion." (paragraph 11, bullet 2)
- ○ B. "'But these amazing plants have had to evolve over thousands of years, developing insect traps to get their nutritional needs met.'" (paragraph 4)
- ○ C. "The traps can be well-disguised to fool the eye, like pitcher plants, which get their name because they look like beautiful pitchers full of nectar." (paragraph 5)
- ○ D. "Hair-like growths along the pitcher walls ensure that nothing can scramble out, and the digestive enzymes can get to work." (paragraph 7)

11. Identify the ways that the plants listed below get their food. Write the sentence in the box that explains how each plant gets their food.

- Uses a sweet nectar
- Closes over bugs to trap them
- Displays a sticky surface
- Sucks in food with water

| Plant | Method for Gathering Food |
|---|---|
| Bladderwort | |
| Pitcher plant | |
| Venus flytrap | |
| Sundews | |

## Answers

### Unit 1: Literary Analysis Task

#### "The Nightingale" and "Old Joe and the Carpenter"

1.  **Part A—(C)** is the correct answer. The lesson in the story is that you have to take care of the things that you like, or they will want to escape, like the Nightingale did. When the Emperor treated the Nightingale well and let her live in the forest, she decided to stay.

    **Part B—(B)** is the correct answer. It shows how the Emperor treated the Nightingale well.

2.  Below is the correct summary that answers the question.

| 1 | The Emperor heard the beautiful singing and asked his servants to find whoever was making the song. |
|---|---|
| 2 | The servants walked and found the bird that was singing. |
| 3 | The Emperor held a feast and everyone listened to the bird sing. |
| 4 | The nightingale escaped and the Emperor became sad when the toy bird broke, because he had no music to listen to. |
| 5 | The nightingale returned to the Emperor, but the Emperor agreed that she could live in the forest. |

3.  **Part A—(D)** is the correct answer. The way the bird looks does not influence her singing. This is similar to the saying, *you can't choose a book by its cover.*

    **Part B—(D)** is the correct answer. Even though the Nightingale was plain looking, she was the best medicine for the Emperor.

4. **Part A—(A)** is the correct answer. The Nightingale was lonely and missed her home in the forest. She missed seeing other birds and animals.

   **Part B—(D)** is the correct answer. This sentence shows that the Nightingale wants to go back and live in her home.

5. **Part A—(C)** is the correct answer. Declined means that he said no to doing the work. Refuse is a synonym of no.

   **Part B—(D)** is the correct answer. The phrase, *had to leave* shows a reason why the carpenter would have refused the work.

6. **(A) and (D)** are two pieces of evidence that describe the setting of the story. The setting is the time and place that the story occurs. Both of these details describe the place where the story happens.

7. **Sample Response**

   The Emperor and Joe are both characters who learn lessons. In "The Nightingale" the Emperor learns that you have to treat the things that you care about well. In "Joe and the Old Carpenter," Joe learns that it is better to build bridges than fences. The character's actions in the stories influence the plot and help the story unfold.

   In "The Nightingale," the Emperor finds a nightingale who sings a beautiful song. The song makes him happy, but his actions make the Nightingale unhappy. The Emperor keeps the Nightingale locked in a cage and she becomes homesick. Because the Emperor is not treating her well, the Nightingale escapes. The Emperor becomes sick and sad when he has no music to listen to. One day the Nightingale returns and the Emperor has learned his lesson. This time he allows the Nightingale to live in the forest. She is much happier, so she visits him often to sing her song.

   In "Joe and the Old Carpenter," Joe learns that it is more important to build bridges than fences. In the story, Joe and his neighbor had an argument. Both men are angry, so the neighbor digs a creek between the two houses so that they can't talk to each other anymore. One day, an old carpenter shows up at Joe's house, and Joe asks him to build a fence around his property. This would keep his neighbor out, and they would not need to see each other. The carpenter has a different plan and builds a bridge. Once the bridge is built, the neighbor comes over and apologizes. The two men become friends again.

Both characters learn important lessons in the stories. Relationships are important and make people happy. Being angry or treating people poorly does not make the characters happy. In both stories, the characters learned that if they changed their actions, they could make their relationships better.

Joe and the Emperor learn ways to solve their problems in both of the stories. In the end, they are both much happier because of the lessons that they have learned. Hopefully they will both live happily ever after!

**"A Stone in the Road"**

8. **Part A—(B)** is the correct answer. Sprawled means to lay on the ground with your arms and legs spread out or askew.

   **Part B—(A)** is the correct answer. The words "rose angrily" gives the reader a clue that supports the definition of sprawled. It indicates that the soldier was on the ground, and then he got up.

9. **Part A—(A)** is the correct answer. The story is about the lesson that the king teaches, it is not about the gold.

   **Part B—(A)** is the correct answer. The king was trying to determine who was lazy and who was not.

10. **Part A—(D)** is the correct answer. Although the phrase *lazy people* is frequently mentioned in the story, the story is mostly about the lesson that the king is trying to teach.

    **Part B—(B)** is the correct answer. The lesson that the king is trying to teach is about solving our own problems.

11. The correct answers are **(A)**, **(E)**, and **(F)**.

12. The correct response is below.

| Character | Response to the Stone in the Road |
|---|---|
| Soldier | Tripped over the stone |
| Farmer | Moved the cart around the stone |
| Young Girl | Moved the rock to the side |

13. The correct answer is below.

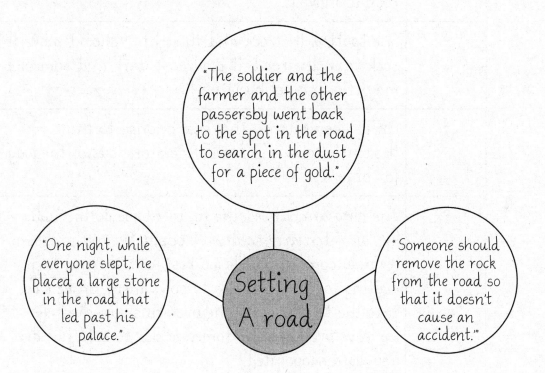

14. Write five sentences from the list below, in the correct order, in the boxes to summarize the story.

| Sequence | Event |
|---|---|
| 1 | One night, while everyone slept, he placed a large stone in the road that led past his palace. He hid at the edge of the road to see what would happen. |
| 2 | All day long the king secretly watched people go around the rock and complain about lazy people leaving the rock in the road; yet no one touched the rock to move it. |
| 3 | She spotted the rock and thought, "I should move this rock from the road; it is almost dark and someone may trip and get hurt." |
| 4 | On it was written, "This box belongs to the thoughtful one who moves the stone out of the way for others." |
| 5 | The king announced the find: "As we go through life, we often are faced with obstacles and problems. We may complain while we just walk around them waiting for someone else to solve them, or we can take the time to solve the problems ourselves. If we leave problems for someone else to solve, we are usually disappointed." |

# Unit 2: Research Simulation Task

1. **Part A—(B)** is the correct answer. An immigrant is someone who is entering a new country.

   **Part B—(A)** is the correct answer. The statement tells about how people came to the United States and supports the definition of the word.

2. **Part A—(C)** is the correct answer. The statement explains how people entered the United States differently. The way they entered was based on their status, or how much money they had.

   **Part B—(B)** is the correct answer. This gives an example of how the steerage passengers were treated when they arrived at Ellis Island.

3. The correct answer is in the chart below.

| Problem | Solution |
|---|---|
| On January 1, 1892, the door to America swung open. | After the ships docked, they were transported to Ellis Island, where everyone would undergo a medical and legal inspection. |
| Doctors would briefly scan every immigrant for obvious physical ailments. | About 2 percent were sent back. Others were held in the island's hospital facilities for long periods of time. |

4. **Part A—(B)** is the correct answer. The Statue of Liberty symbolizes freedom in the United States, which means that the United States is a country where people can make their own choices.

   **Part B—(C)** is the correct answer. This detail supports the answer to Part A.

5. **Part A—(C)** is the correct answer. It best summarizes the story.

   **Part B—(C) and (D)** are details that support the main idea of the story. The other details are not as important and do not directly support the main idea.

6.  **Part A—(D)** is the correct answer. The author tells about the Statue of Liberty in chronological order.

    **Part B—(D)** is the correct answer. This answer supports that the author has organized the story chronologically starting with very early details about how the Statue of Liberty became a symbol of the United States.

7.  **Part A—(B)** is the correct answer. Native means that it is something that has always lived in a certain area. Bald Eagles have always lived in the United States.

    **Part B—(D)** is the correct answer. This answer gives an example that supports the fact that Bald Eagles live across the United States.

8.  **Part A—(B)** is the correct answer. This is the best reason why the Bald Eagle was selected as a symbol of our country.

    **Part B—(D)** is the correct answer. This provides an example that supports the answer to Part A.

9.  **Sample Response**

    Between 1892 and 1954, twelve million immigrants came into the United States through New York City. Immigrants came to America for many reasons, but mostly for the freedom that the country offered them. This freedom allows them to make their own choices about religion and how they want to live. America has many symbols that represent this freedom. Three of these symbols are Ellis Island, the Statue of Liberty, and the Bald Eagle. Of these three symbols, the Statue of Liberty is the most important symbol of this freedom.

    Ellis Island was the doorway to America. When immigrants arrived by boat, their first stop was Ellis Island. Only poor passengers had to go through the screening process at Ellis Island. The screening process was designed to identify anyone that was sick or might be a criminal. Some people were sent back to their countries, while others were held at Ellis Island until they were no longer sick. Once the immigrants were cleared, they were allowed to enter into the country.

Before the immigrants got to Ellis Island, they were greeted by the Statue of Liberty. The statue is a symbol of freedom for the United States and was a gift from France. The Statue is made of copper and stands 115 feet high in New York Harbor. It is located next to Ellis Island.

The third symbol is the Bald Eagle. The Bald Eagle is a bird that is native to the United States and it is found across the country. The eagle flies fast and is beautiful. It represents beauty and independence, which are foundations that this county is built on. The eagle was once endangered, but since it is a national symbol, they are now protected, and the numbers are slowly growing.

Of these three symbols, the Statue of Liberty is the most powerful, especially for immigrants arriving in the country. The Statue was the first symbol of freedom that many immigrants saw. The shackles at the base of her feet represent freedom from slavery, and the seven spikes in her crown represent the seven continents. The immigrants had endured such a long, hard voyage; the Statue was a welcome site that told them they were home. Unlike Ellis Island, which probably inspired fear due to the long process and chance of being sent home, the Statue of Liberty represented hope for their new life in the United States.

The United States of America has many symbols that represent its heritage. Three of these symbols are Ellis Island, the Statue of Liberty, and the Bald Eagle. All represent freedom, which was an important reason that immigrants came to America. Of these three symbols, the Statue of Liberty is probably the most powerful. The United States of America is a land of great opportunity!

## Unit 3: Narrative Writing Task

### "A Fairy Story: An Excerpt from *Rebecca of Sunnybrook Farm*"

1. **Part A—(A)** is the correct answer. Paragraph two gives details about the setting. The setting is where the story takes place.

   **Part B—(B)** is the correct answer. This sentence provides details that reflect the setting that is presented in paragraph 2.

2. **Part A—(B)** is the correct answer. The Fairy Godmother was concerned that the Princess was tired from plowing the fields.

   **Part B—(B)** is the correct answer. This paragraph explains that the Princess was tired when she saw her Fairy Godmother.

3. **Part A—(A)** is the correct answer. The Princess is thankful for the rest that she was able to get because of the Fairy Godmother's actions.

   **Part B—(C)** is the correct answer. This detail shows how the Princess tried to thank the Fairy Godmother many times for her help.

4. **Part A—(C)** is the correct answer. The Princess is hardworking because, even though her work is hard, she never quits.

   **Part B—(C) and (E)** are the correct answers. Both of these details support how hard the Princess worked.

5. **Sample Response**

   Clomp, Clomp, Clomp. The horse's hooves struck the ground as the Fairy Godmother's carriage moved quickly down the road. The Fairy Godmother was headed to the King's court when she saw a tired looking princess by the side of the road at her cottage. The Fairy Godmother could see that the princess had spent the day using a heavy plow to tend to her field.

   "If you are tired, poor little Princess, why do you not go into the cool green forest and rest?"

   The princess explained that she did not have time and needed to keep working her field so that she would have an abundant harvest. The Fairy Godmother felt badly for the princess, and the King sensed this. In his own quiet way, the king encouraged the Fairy Godmother to move forward with a plan to help the princess.

Each day, the Fairy Godmother found a strong man and paid him a sack of gold coins. The man would then go and plow for the princess. Each day, the Fairy Godmother would drive by the cottage in her chariot, and would be pleased to see the princess in the cool forest instead of in the hot field.

A few days went by and the Fairy Godmother began finding leaves that had words poked into them by a needle. The Fairy Godmother smiled, pleased that the princess was unburdened and able to spread her thoughts throughout the kingdom. As more time passed, the Fairy Godmother found many more leaves, many more than the princess alone could have made. The Fairy Godmother knew that her work had spread joy to many others, and that made her very happy. She had hoped to make the princess's life better, but along the way had spread joy to many other people, and that was the best gift of all.

### "Chomp! Meat-Eating Plants"

6.  **Part A—(B)** is the correct answer. A carnivore is a meat eater.

    **Part B—(A)** is the correct answer. It shows how the plant eats meat.

7.  **Part A—(B)** is the correct answer. This is the main idea of the text.

    **Part B—(C)** is the correct answer. This detail provides an example of how plants trap their food.

8.  **Part A—(A)** is the correct answer. The bladderwort is sneaky because it appears to be a harmless plant.

    **Part B—(A)** is the correct answer. Another detail about the bladderwort is that it eats mosquito eggs.

9.  **Part A—(A)** is the correct answer. The information is presented as a problem, and then the author discusses how the plants have overcome the problem.

    **Part B—(B)** is the correct answer. This detail shows the problem in the story.

10. **Part A—(D)** is the correct answer. The problem in the article is that the plants needed to find other ways to get nutrition.

**Part B—(B)** is the correct answer. The solution to the problem presented in Part A is that the plants have changed to get their nutritional needs in other ways.

11. The correct answer is below.

| Plant | Method for Gathering Food |
|---|---|
| Bladderwort | Sucks in food with water |
| Pitcher plant | Uses a sweet nectar |
| Venus flytrap | Closes over bugs to trap them |
| Sundews | Displays a sticky surface |

> **REMINDER:** Changes to the format, style, and questions are ongoing. Continue to check the PARCC website for up-to-date changes and information.

## Unit 1

### Literary Analysis Task

Read the excerpts from "Cheddar's Tales: Crisis in Crittertown" and answer the questions that follow. Then write an essay based on the prompt.

### Excerpts from *Cheddar's Tales*

#### *Crisis in Crittertown*

#### By Justine Fontes

### The Change

1   Before The Change, my thoughts were few and simple: Don't get killed. Find food—hopefully cheese!

2   Back then I didn't even know what cheese was. I just liked to eat it more than anything else. I didn't know what a cow was, and I certainly had no clue about the chemicals that transform milk into the world's greatest food.

3   My knowledge barely reached beyond the basement of the post office in Crittertown, Maine, where my colony and I struggled to keep one jump ahead of hunger, cold, cats, brooms, and other disasters. People and all their amazing inventions meant only two things to us: food and danger. Then suddenly, one October day, everything changed.

**4** The music started making sense. That's what I remember first. Music always sounded nice. But then there was that magical morning, when the songs on the radio suddenly had lyrics I could understand. It wasn't just mood and beat. The words made sense!

**5** Everyone else in the colony felt it, too. Our minds sprang to life with words and ideas. We wondered what was happening! Was it only happening to us or to mice everywhere? Then a cricket chirped, "What's going on?" We wondered if it was happening to every critter.

**6** Thanks to birds, word of The Change spread quickly. Birds get around and they gossip. The birds said it was occurring all around human talking machines, like telephones, radios, and TVs. No critter knew why. We only knew that suddenly we understood human babble—and there was a lot of it!

**7** Most of us felt like we'd snapped awake during a thrilling movie that might end in a happily-ever-after or a terrible tragedy. And we weren't just watching the movie. We were characters with an important part to play.

**8** Before The Change, mice didn't have names. We knew each other by smell, sight, and relationships. After it, we quickly came up with names for ourselves—or each other.

**9** Every mouse called me Cheddar because I'm crazy for cheese, especially that sharp, tangy delight known as cheddar. My best friend is the grandson of our leader, and his father is a handsome shade of gray. Therefore, my friend became Grayson. Maybe he'll grow into that dignified name someday. The Grayson I know is a hothead, always rushing into danger.

**10** The morning of The Change was no different. As soon as we realized we could understand humans, Grayson squeaked, "We must explore! Let's go upstairs and find out what they do at the post office."

**11** Up until then we didn't know zip about zip codes. All we knew about the postal service was when the workers came and went, and what they left in the trash cans.

**12** "No one's going anywhere!" our leader squeaked firmly. Brownback was a cautious mouse. Like his son, he was mostly gray, but with a stripe of brown down his back. His muzzle fur was white with age. We all respected him greatly—except Grayson.

**13** "Ah, Pops! There's so much to learn. It could benefit the colony. I'll be careful," Grayson promised. "I won't make a sound or let anyone see me. I'll . . . even take Cheddar along."

**14** To my surprise, this last phrase changed Brownback's expression.

**15** Grayson saw that, too, because he squeaked on. "He'll keep me in line. You know Cheddar. He's always holding me back from fun . . . I mean danger."

**16** Brownback nodded. "Cheddar is cautious, and caution keeps a mouse alive."

**17** I felt flattered. "Cautious" sounds so much better than "coward."

**18** Grayson seized on this. "We won't stay long. We'll come home with lots of news for you."

**19** Brownback always said, "Facts help a leader make good decisions." He liked news almost as much as I like cheese. Brownback nodded. "You and Cheddar may go upstairs." Grayson jumped so high, even his tail left the ground.

**20** Brownback sighed. "Calm down, boy." Then he told me, "Don't let him do anything foolish."

**21** I nodded, suddenly realizing what had happened. What happened?! When had I agreed to go upstairs?

1. Write the sentences in the boxes below to create a summary of "The Change."

   - The mice gave each other names.

   - The mice started to understand human language.

   - Brownback agreed to let Grayson go exploring, as long as Cheddar went with him.

   - The mice got ready to go upstairs and learn about the world.

   - Grayson wanted to go exploring, but Brownback said No.

---

**First**

---

**Second**

---

**Third**

---

**Fourth**

---

**Fifth**

2. **Part A**

Read the following sentence from paragraph 3 of "Cheddar's Tales: Crisis in Crittertown."

> My knowledge barely reached beyond the basement of the post office in Crittertown, Maine, where my **colony** and I struggled to keep one jump ahead of hunger, cold, cats, brooms, and other disasters.

What does the word **colony** mean as it is used in this sentence?

○   A.   a group of people sent out by a state/country to create a new territory

○   B.   a group of plants or animals that live together

○   C.   a mass of microbes

○   D.   a group of people with common interests

**Part B**

Which sentence from the story **best** supports your choice in Part A.

○   A.   "'No one's going anywhere!' our leader squeaked firmly." (paragraph 12)

○   B.   "Before The Change, mice didn't have names. We knew each other by smell, sight, and relationships." (paragraph 8)

○   C.   "All we knew about the postal service was when the workers came and went, and what they left in the trash cans." (paragraph 11)

○   D.   "He liked news almost as much as I like cheese." (paragraph 19)

3. **Part A**

How does Brownback feel about Cheddar? He thinks that Cheddar
is _____.

○ A. brave

○ B. foolish

○ C. cowardly

○ D. careful

**Part B**

Which sentence **best** shows how his feelings about Cheddar impact his
decision to let the mice go exploring?

○ A. "Brownback nodded. 'Cheddar is cautious, and caution keeps a
mouse alive.'" (paragraph 16)

○ B. "Brownback was a cautious mouse." (paragraph 12)

○ C. "He liked news almost as much as I like cheese." (paragraph 19)

○ D. "'No one's going anywhere!' our leader squeaked firmly."
(paragraph 12)

## The Journey

**1**  This was even scarier than the time Grayson talked me into helping him use a pencil to trip a trap. I shuddered at that memory. How did I let him get me into these things?

**2**  The first part of our journey was familiar. Grayson and I often visited the parking lot shared by the post office and the Crittertown Market. But we always did this at night when there were no cars or trucks zooming around.

**3**  We watched the cars come and go. How busy everything was during the day!

**4**  People carried bags out of the market, and packages to or from the post office. I squeaked, "They buy food at the market. What do they do at the post office?"

**5**  "Let's find out!" Grayson replied. Then he slid under the torn rubber trim at the bottom of the post office's rickety back door.

**6**  I looked around the parking lot. Staying there alone was almost as scary as following Grayson. Besides, I'd promised Brownback to keep both eyes on his grandson. I scurried under the door after my friend.

**7**  We caught our breath in the back room with the coats. We sniffed and listened. I smelled the postmaster's coffee and the clerk's perfume. I heard the radio playing the "morning mix" of love songs, news, and trivia.

**8**  Grayson tapped my shoulder and then slinked into the office itself. What choice did I have? Once again, I followed my friend into unknown danger.

**9**  Looking around, I found I could read human writing! Posters urged the mail carriers to "Buckle up for safety" and "Watch out for children! School is open."

**10**  "What's school?" I asked.

**11** Grayson shrugged.

**12** Slowly some things started making sense. Mail turned out to be letters, catalogs, magazines, and packages. Packages contained all kinds of things: big, small, valuable, and some "just old baby clothes I'm sending to my sister."

**13** Grayson and I gradually grasped the postal basics. Workers delivered mail to the people of Crittertown and sent mail from Crittertown to humans elsewhere. Some of those places were very far away.

**14** Before long, Grayson and I felt stuffed with facts. How could we remember them all?

**15** I suggested, "Let's report to your grandfather."

**16** Grayson argued, "Let's learn more."

**17** So we stayed until the mail carriers left on their routes. The carriers were the people who drove the mail to all the homes and businesses in Crittertown.

**18** We watched the postmaster do his morning reports on the computer. Grayson crept closer to find out what this machine did. He whispered, "It sends messages. It records and calculates numbers."

**19** Numbers counted how much you had of something, and they were used in addresses, like the 1, 2, 3, third house on Berry Lane.

**20** I felt smart, but also hungry. "Can't we go home?"

**21** Grayson looked annoyed. "Don't you want to see the rest of the post office? Didn't you hear the Clerk mention the snack table?"

**22** Grayson knew me too well. While the postmaster stared at his computer, we slinked to the front of the office.

**23** I couldn't smell cheese, but I sensed its presence. Maybe cheese sends out a frequency, like a TV broadcast. Maybe my stomach is tuned to the cheese channel.

**24** Grayson and I scrambled up a stack of Priority Mail boxes to the tabletop. We saw a heap of plastic-wrapped treasures labeled cheese sandwich crackers. My mouth watered and my gut growled. "We shouldn't," I cautioned.

**25** Grayson chuckled. "We shouldn't, but we will and you know it!"

**26** While the postmaster talked on the phone, we eased open the nearest package. Oh, that wonderful smell! Grayson tugged the top cracker out of the wrapper. By the time we finished that first orange disk, I decided the post office was the greatest place in the world!

**27** Grayson wanted to stay all day. But I convinced him to leave when Mike went to lunch. I said, "We can come back tomorrow. This way, Brownback will see you're being cautious." Then I added, "If we stay too long, every mouse will worry and Brownback might not let us out again." That did it. We slipped under the door and into the parking lot and headed home.

**28** Our nervous friend, Twitchy, spotted us first. He squeaked, "They're here!"

**29** Twitchy sniffed our noses and then squealed. "It's really you! You're okay!"

**30** Brownback stepped forward. "I was just starting to worry."

**31** I winked at Grayson. He winked back.

**4. Part A**

Read the following sentence from paragraph 22 of "The Journey."

> While the postmaster stared at his computer, we **slinked** to the front of the office.

What does the word **slinked** mean as it is used in this sentence?

- ○  A.  to spring back and forth
- ○  B.  to run quickly
- ○  C.  to jump
- ○  D.  to move sneakily

**Part B**

Why does the author choose to use the word slinked?

- ○  A.  because mice are loud
- ○  B.  because the mice needed to be careful to not get caught
- ○  C.  because the mice didn't want to get stepped on
- ○  D.  because the floors were creaky in the post office

**5.** Write a word from the list in the boxes below that **best** describes the characters in "The Change" and "The Journey."

Spoiled     Daring     Trustworthy     Fair     Kind

| Name | Character Trait |
|---|---|
| Cheddar | |
| Grayson | |
| Brownback | |

6. **Part A**

   Which statement **best** describes how Cheddar feels about the post office
   when he first arrives?

   ○ A. He felt overwhelmed by many smells and noises.
   ○ B. He felt scared because he sees a cat.
   ○ C. He felt hungry because he could sense cheese.
   ○ D. He felt concerned about getting back to the colony.

   **Part B**

   Which sentence from the passage **best** supports your answer to Part A.

   ○ A. "I squeaked, 'They buy food at the market. What do they do at the
        post office?'" (paragraph 4)
   ○ B. "I smelled the postmaster's coffee and the clerk's perfume. I heard
        the radio playing the 'morning mix' of love songs, news, and trivia."
        (paragraph 7)
   ○ C. "Before long, Grayson and I felt stuffed with facts." (paragraph 14)
   ○ D. "Maybe my stomach is tuned to the cheese channel." (paragraph 23)

7. In both "The Change" and "The Journey," Cheddar goes on interesting
   adventures that reveal information about his character. Name two character
   traits that describe Cheddar and provide evidence from the stories to support
   the character traits.

   ---------------------------------------------------------------

   ---------------------------------------------------------------

   ---------------------------------------------------------------

   ---------------------------------------------------------------

   ---------------------------------------------------------------

   ---------------------------------------------------------------

## In a Class by Himself

### by Tamara Lauriano

1   The first day my new teacher walked into our school in Spanish Harlem, I burst out laughing. Ron Clark was this young white guy from North Carolina who talked with a funny Southern accent. He said he used to be a singing waiter. I thought, who is this guy? He's a complete joke.

2   It was 1999, and I was in the fifth grade at New York City's P.S. 83. I figured I'd spend most of the year in the principal's office. I'd always been a troublemaker. I'd get yelled at, and then the teachers would give up on me. I thought that's what would happen with Ron Clark.

3   I was wrong. That first week, I kept mocking him. He hauled me out to the hallway and said I'd better shape up. "Tamara," he said, "you're a smart kid. You can do better."

4   He told me I was a natural leader and that I'd go far in life if I started applying myself. I was mad at first, but then something happened: I began to respect him. There were 29 students in our class, and it didn't take long for us to realize that Ron Clark was no ordinary teacher.

5   He was only 27 and had the most unusual way of teaching. To help us learn the states and capitals, he changed the lyrics of a popular rap hit and had us sing and dance with him. When we read the Harry Potter books, he decorated our classroom like Hogwarts. And during the Presidential election, he put campaign posters on the walls and covered the room with 5,000 red, white, and blue stars.

6   Like most teachers, he had lots of rules: Treat each other like family. Don't butt in line. But the real difference was how involved he was.   Mr. Clark ate with us in the lunchroom

instead of going to the teachers' lounge. At first, my friends and I were thinking, what is he doing?

7    He asked us what was going on in our lives. At recess, he came outside with us, and we taught him how to jump rope. When it snowed, Mr. Clark, who'd never seen snow before, pelted us with snowballs, and we pelted him back.

8    Before coming to P.S. 83, he taught at Snowden Elementary in his hometown, Belhaven, North Carolina. His parents were DJs at dance clubs, so he grew up with music and energy. He wanted a life of adventure, he told me, but his mom encouraged him to apply for a position at Snowden when one of the teachers passed away. Mr. Clark ended up loving it. He came to Harlem because he'd seen a TV show about our troubled schools and the lack of qualified teachers. He wanted a challenge. Boy, did he get one.

9    When I met him, I had a lot of anger inside of me. I've lived my whole life in Spanish Harlem with my mom, grandmother, and little sister, Ivy. I never had a father, but in my neighborhood that's not unusual. You have to watch yourself. There are shoot-ups all the time. I know kids who have been shot or beaten up. I have friends who ended up in jail or pregnant. I could have ended up that way, too, but Mr. Clark and my mom wouldn't let that happen.

10    Mr. Clark worked long hours, making sure I did my work. My grades rose. In fact, our whole fifth-grade class's scores rose in math and reading. In sixth grade, I entered the gifted program, and Mr. Clark was the teacher. I felt so lucky to have him for a second year!

11    He took our class to see *The Phantom of the Opera*, and it was the first time some kids had ever been out of Harlem. Before the show, he treated us to dinner at a restaurant and taught us not to talk with our mouths full—stuff you don't usually learn

in the ghetto. He told us to say "Yes, ma'am" and "No, sir." We didn't want to let him down.

12    None of us were surprised when Mr. Clark was selected as Disney's 2000 Teacher of the Year. When he learned he'd won, he said he would draw three names out of a hat; those students would go with him to Los Angeles to get the award. But when it came time to draw names, Mr. Clark said, "You're all going."

13    He got donations to fly all 37 of us out to Disneyland in California and put us up at the Hilton. We were there for three days. People were amazed, but Mr. Clark really cared about us. There's no way I can imagine most teachers doing that. No way. But he saw something in us that nobody else saw.

14    On graduation day, there were a lot of tears. We didn't want his class to end. Was I ever surprised when Mr. Clark showed up at my new junior high the first week of school, just to say hello. He's been a constant in our lives. In 2001, he moved to Atlanta, but he always kept in touch. He started giving speeches about education, and wrote a best-selling book based on his classroom rules, *The Essential 55.*

15    In 2003, Mr. Clark took some of us on a trip to South Africa to deliver school supplies and visit orphanages. It was the most amazing experience of my life. It's now my dream to one day start a group of women's clubs, helping people from all backgrounds.

16    I'm about to become a senior at Harlem Renaissance High School. My grades are beautiful now, and I'm hoping to go to law school eventually. This fall, Mr. Clark will be opening the Ron Clark Academy in Atlanta, a school for kids who have potential but aren't reaching it. Kids who are like I was—until Mr. Clark came along.

8. **Part A**

What is the author's purpose for writing this article?

- ○  A.  to entertain us with stories of why Mr. Clark won the Disney Teacher of the Year Award
- ○  B.  to persuade us that Mr. Clark was a complete joke
- ○  C.  to express her feelings that a caring teacher can make a difference in the life of his or her students
- ○  D.  to inform us how successful she has become

**Part B**

Which sentence from the story "In a Class by Himself" **best** supports the answer to Part A?

- ○  A.  "Kids who are like I was—until Mr. Clark came along." (paragraph 16)
- ○  B.  "None of us were surprised when Mr. Clark was selected as Disney's 2000 Teacher of the Year." (paragraph 12)
- ○  C.  "In 2003, Mr. Clark took some of us on a trip to South Africa to deliver school supplies and visit orphanages." (paragraph 15)
- ○  D.  "When we read the Harry Potter books, he decorated our classroom like Hogwarts." (paragraph 5)

9. **Part A**

Read the following sentence from paragraph 7 of "In a Class by Himself."

"Mr. Clark, who'd never seen snow before, **pelted** us with snowballs."

What does the word **pelted** mean as it is used in this sentence?

- ○  A.  hurled or threw
- ○  B.  protected
- ○  C.  helped
- ○  D.  bribed

**Part B**

Which word(s) from the sentence **best** helps you determine the meaning of the word **pelted**?

- ○ A. Mr. Clark
- ○ B. never seen snow
- ○ C. us
- ○ D. snowballs

10. **Part A**

Which answer best summarizes the author's feelings about Mr. Clark?

- ○ A. He was a fun teacher.
- ○ B. He won many awards.
- ○ C. He worked hard.
- ○ D. He changed her life for the better.

**Part B**

What evidence from the story **best** supports your answer to Part A?

- ○ A. "He wanted a challenge. Boy, did he get one." (paragraph 8)
- ○ B. "He started giving speeches about education, and wrote a best-selling book based on his classroom rules, *The Essential 55*." (paragraph 14)
- ○ C. "My grades are beautiful now, and I'm hoping to go to law school eventually." (paragraph 16)
- ○ D. "This fall, Mr. Clark will be opening the Ron Clark Academy in Atlanta, a school for kids who have potential but aren't reaching it." (paragraph 16)

11. Select two character traits below that describe Mr. Clark and write them in Column 1. Then select a sentence from the text in the list below that provides evidence for the character trait and write it in Column 2.

**Character Traits**

Compassionate
Competitive
Sociable
Ambitious
Curious

**Evidence**

- "I was wrong. That first week, I kept mocking him. He hauled me out to the hallway and said I'd better shape up. 'Tamara,' he said, 'you're a smart kid. You can do better.'" (paragraph 3)

- "Mr. Clark ate with us in the lunchroom instead of going to the teachers' lounge." (paragraph 6)

- "In 2003, Mr. Clark took some of us on a trip to South Africa to deliver school supplies and visit orphanages." (paragraph 15)

- "He came to Harlem because he'd seen a TV show about our troubled schools and the lack of qualified teachers. He wanted a challenge. Boy, did he get one." (paragraph 8)

- "On graduation day, there were a lot of tears. We didn't want his class to end." (paragraph 14)

| Column 1 Character Trait | Column 2 Evidence |
|---|---|
|  |  |
|  |  |

**12.** Write the responses below in the chart that show the way that Mr. Clark responds to the events in the story. Not all responses will be used.

- "He told me I was a natural leader and that I'd go far in life if I started applying myself." (paragraph 4)

- "In 2003, Mr. Clark took some of us on a trip to South Africa to deliver school supplies and visit orphanages." (paragraph 15)

- "This fall, Mr. Clark will be opening the Ron Clark Academy in Atlanta, a school for kids who have potential but aren't reaching it." (paragraph 16)

- "Mr. Clark worked long hours, making sure I did my work." (paragraph 10)

- "But when it came time to draw names, Mr. Clark said, 'You're all going.'" (paragraph 12)

- "He's been a constant in our lives. In 2001, he moved to Atlanta, but he always kept in touch." (paragraph 14)

| Event | Supporting Detail |
|---|---|
| Tamara is acting up in class. | |
| The students needed to improve their grades. | |
| Mr. Clark wins the Disney Teacher of the Year Award. | |

# Unit 2

## Research Simulation Task

Read the articles about surviving in the wilderness. There are two articles and one table included as sources for the task. Then write an essay based on the prompt that follows.

### Lost! Survival in the Wilderness

1 What if you were walking in the woods alone and got lost? What would you do? When you realize that you are lost, you might start to panic. Take a deep breath and stop. Think about what is happening and observe your surroundings. Once you have thought about the problem, create a plan to stay safe.

2 The most important thing to do is to stay in one place. If you are lost, it will be hard to find your way out. As soon as someone realizes that you are missing, they will begin a search. If you stay in one place, it will be much easier for someone to find you. It also reduces the risk of you being injured. If you are with a group of people, be sure to stay together.

3 The most important things that you need to do while waiting for rescue is to maintain your body temperature, conserve energy, drink water, and attract attention (if possible).

4 You can maintain your body temperature in different ways. If it is cold, you need to stay warm. You can find shelter, use a blanket, etc. Trees can help break the wind or protect you from snow or rain. If it is hot, look for shade to stay cool.

5 Your body will need water more than it needs food. Look for water around where you are lost. Drinking from a spring is generally safe. If you are going to drink from a river or pond, it is best to boil the water for at least 10 minutes before you drink it. This will only work if you are able to build a fire. If you cannot build a fire, you can strain the water through your shirt or some other material. This will help remove anything that might make you sick. A final option is to collect rainwater or morning dew as drinking water.

6   Finally, it is important to attract attention if you can. Carrying a whistle is important when you are going out into the wilderness. A whistle is an effective signaling tool that will help searchers find you. Three short blasts is a known signal for help. In addition, try using rocks, branches, or sticks to draw an X or an SOS on the ground. If you hear a helicopter, wave your arms. Hold a flag or bright colored fabric in your hand to help anyone see you from the air.

7   The best way to stay safe if you become lost in the wilderness is to prepare before you go. Let someone know where you are going, and when you expect to return. Water, a brightly colored bandana, and a flashlight are also important tools to have. A few garbage bags in your pack can also be used as a blanket, a tarp, or a water collection device. Matches and a pocket knife can also be helpful additions to your pack.

8   Getting lost can be scary. It is important to remember these survival tips and to stay calm. Find water, seek shelter, and stay in one place. If you follow these tips, and prepare before you go, rescue should come and you will stay safe.

1. **Part A**

Read the following sentence from paragraph 3 from "Lost! Survival in the Wilderness."

> The most important things that you need to do while waiting for rescue is to maintain your body temperature, **conserve** energy, drink water, and attract attention (if possible).

What is the meaning of the word **conserve** as it is used in the sentence?

- ○ A. keep safe
- ○ B. recycle
- ○ C. save
- ○ D. create

**Part B**

Which sentence **best** supports your answer to Part A.

- ○ A. "Once you have thought about the problem, create a plan to stay safe." (paragraph 1)
- ○ B. "If it is cold, you need to stay warm." (paragraph 4)
- ○ C. "The most important thing to do is to stay in one place." (paragraph 2)
- ○ D. "Carrying a whistle is important when you are going out into the wilderness." (paragraph 6)

2. **Part A**

Why is it important to plan before you go out into the wilderness?

- ○ A. You will be able to stay calm.
- ○ B. You can find water more easily.
- ○ C. You can bring supplies that will help you in an emergency.
- ○ D. You can build a shelter.

**Part B**

Which sentence from the text **best** supports your answer to Part A?

- ○ A. "Water, a brightly colored bandana, and a flashlight are also important tools to have." (paragraph 7)
- ○ B. "The most important thing to do is to stay in one place." (paragraph 2)
- ○ C. "If it is cold, you need to stay warm." (paragraph 4)
- ○ D. "It is important to remember these survival tips and to stay calm." (paragraph 8)

3. **Part A**

   Which alternate title **best** expresses the main idea of the text from "Lost! Survival in the Wilderness"?

   ○  A.  Building a Shelter in the Forest
   ○  B.  How to Make Water Safe for Boiling
   ○  C.  Hug a Tree
   ○  D.  Planning Before You Go Is the Key to Safety

   **Part B**

   Which two sentences from the text **best** support your answer to Part A?

   ☐  A.  "The most important thing to do is to stay in one place." (paragraph 2)
   ☐  B.  "Take a deep breath and stop." (paragraph 1)
   ☐  C.  "A few garbage bags in your pack can also be used as a blanket, a tarp, or a water collection device." (paragraph 7)
   ☐  D.  "If you hear a helicopter, wave your arms." (paragraph 6)
   ☐  E.  "The best way to stay safe if you become lost in the wilderness is to prepare before you go." (paragraph 7)
   ☐  F.  "Your body will need water more than it needs food." (paragraph 5)

# Survival Essentials

---

**This article contains safety information about going on an expedition in the wilderness.**

---

**1** Water: You need water to survive, but beware. Water from streams and rivers could be polluted and make you ill. You must boil it before you drink it.

**2** Protein: Your muscles need protein to make them strong. Meat, eggs, cheese, and nuts are good sources of protein.

**3** Carbohydrates: Your body needs sugar for energy, and it gets it from carbohydrates. Rice and pasta are good to eat before an expedition. Grain bars are great snacks. Never eat something you don't recognize. Lots of plants, berries, and fungi (mushrooms) are poisonous.

**4** Wild animals might be unwelcome companions on an expedition, but you can't really blame them. After all, you're in their territory!

**5** **ANIMAL SURVIVAL TIPS**

- Blow a whistle if you're walking in bear country. *Why? Bears avoid loud noises.*

- Don't suck the poison out of someone else's snake bite. *Why? The poison may work on you.*

- If you get bitten by a poisonous animal, keep still while you wait for help. *Why? Moving makes poison flow faster through your body.*

- Avoid animals with their young. *Why? They may attack to protect their babies.*

- If you meet a grizzly bear, climb a tree. *Why? Grizzlies can't climb trees, but remember that black bears can.*

**6**   While on your expedition, you have to be prepared for a range of small but scary critters! Here's a nightmare checklist.

**7**   Snakes: There are hundreds of different kinds of poisonous snakes in the world. The most deadly land snakes live in Australia and can kill in minutes.

**8**   Scorpions: Scorpions have a stinger in their tail. The most dangerous live in the Sahara Desert in Africa and can cause serious illness. They tend to hide in dark, shadowy places such as shoes and sleeping bags.

**9**   Spiders: The world's most poisonous spiders are the funnel-web spiders found in Australia, and the brown recluse spiders found in the U.S. Both can cause serious illness.

**10**   Parasitic Worms: A nasty range of tiny parasites can be ingested by unwary travelers who drink or eat contaminated water or food. They live inside the body, and can make their host very ill.

**11**   After that loathsome list, do you still want to go traveling? Before you go, check out what kind of crazy creatures you might face.

**12**   Expedition Tip: Creepy crawlies are often timid, and if you don't surprise them, they are less likely to attack.

## 4. Part A

Read the following sentence from paragraph 4 of "Survival Essentials."

> Wild animals might be unwelcome companions on an **expedition**, but you can't really blame them.

What is the meaning of the word **expedition** as it is used in this sentence?

- ○ A. move quickly
- ○ B. a group
- ○ C. friends
- ○ D. a trip

## Part B

What word gives the **best** clue to the meaning of the word expedition?

- ○ A. companions
- ○ B. blame
- ○ C. territory
- ○ D. animals

## 5. Part A

What is the author's purpose for writing "Survival Essentials"?

- ○ A. to entertain the reader with interesting facts
- ○ B. to inform the reader how to stay safe in the wilderness
- ○ C. to persuade the reader to go on an expedition
- ○ D. to describe the animals in the wilderness

## Part B

Which sentence from the story **best** supports your answer to Part A.

- ○ A. "The most deadly land snakes live in Australia and can kill in minutes." (paragraph 7)
- ○ B. "You must boil it before you drink it." (paragraph 1)
- ○ C. "Here's a nightmare checklist." (paragraph 6)
- ○ D. "After that loathsome list, do you still want to go traveling?" (paragraph 11)

**6.** How are the texts "Lost! Survival in the Wilderness" and "Survival Essentials" similar? Select three reasons from the list below.

☐ A. Both texts state that planning before you go into the wilderness is important.

☐ B. Both texts give detailed information about different types of animals that you might encounter.

☐ C. Both texts state that water is essential to survival.

☐ D. Both texts state that you should stay where you are if you become lost in the woods.

☐ E. Both texts state that you should not go into the wilderness.

☐ F. Both texts state that a whistle can be useful.

**How Long Can You Survive Without the Things That You Need?**

| Air | 3 minutes |
|-----|-----------|
| Shelter | 3 hours (in harsh weather—snow, cold, rain) |
| Water | 3 days |
| Food | 3 weeks |

**7.** Considering all three texts, write the statements in the true or false boxes.

- You should not be concerned with animals in the wild.

- Water found in nature should be boiled before it is consumed.

- Bad weather requires you to find shelter quickly.

- You should walk around and try and find your way out if you become lost.

- You will need to find water more quickly than food.

| True | False |
|------|-------|
|      |       |

8. **Research Simulation Task**

You have read three texts about survival in the wilderness. Write a how-to essay that describes how someone can stay safe while they are waiting for help, if they become lost in the wilderness. Be sure to use facts and details from all three texts in your essay.

The three texts are:

- Lost! Survival in the Wilderness

- Survival Essentials

- How Long Can You Survive Without the Things That You Need? (Table)

-------------------------------------------------------------------

-------------------------------------------------------------------

-------------------------------------------------------------------

-------------------------------------------------------------------

-------------------------------------------------------------------

-------------------------------------------------------------------

-------------------------------------------------------------------

-------------------------------------------------------------------

-------------------------------------------------------------------

-------------------------------------------------------------------

-------------------------------------------------------------------

# Unit 3

## Narrative Writing Task

Today you will read a folktale about a boy named Ping. As you read the story, think about the details the author uses, as you will be asked to write your own story.

Read "The Empty Pot." Then answer the questions.

### The Empty Pot
### by Demi

1   A long time ago in China there was a boy named Ping who loved flowers. Anything he planted burst into bloom. Up came flowers, bushes, and even big fruit trees, as if by magic.

2   Everyone in the kingdom loved flowers too. They planted them everywhere, and the air smelled like perfume. The Emperor loved birds and animals, but flowers most of all and he tended his own garden every day. But the Emperor was very old. He needed to choose a successor to the throne.

3   Who would his successor be? And how would the Emperor choose? Because the Emperor loved flowers so much, he decided to let the flowers choose.

4   The next day a proclamation was issued: All the children in the land were to come to the palace. There they would be given special flower seeds by the Emperor. "Whoever can show me their best in a year's time," he said, "will succeed me to the throne."

5   This news created great excitement throughout the land! Children from all over the country swarmed to the palace to get their flower seeds. All the parents wanted their children to be chosen Emperor, and all the children hoped they would be chosen too!

**6**  When Ping received his seed from the Emperor, he was the happiest child of all. He was sure he could grow the most beautiful flower. Ping filled a flowerpot with rich soil. He planted the seed in it very carefully. He watered it every day. He couldn't wait to see it sprout, grow, and blossom into a beautiful flower!

**7**  Day after day passed, but nothing grew in his pot. Ping was very worried. He put new soil into a bigger pot. Then he transferred the seed into the rich black soil. Another two months he waited. Still nothing happened. By and by the whole year passed.

**8**  Spring came, and all the children put on their best clothes to greet the Emperor. They rushed to the palace with their beautiful flowers, eagerly hoping to be chosen.

**9**  Ping was ashamed of his empty pot. He thought the other children would laugh at him because for once he couldn't get a flower to grow. His clever friend ran by, holding a great big plant.

"Ping!" he said. "You're not really going to the Emperor with an empty pot, are you? Couldn't you grow a great flower like mine?"

10   "I've grown lots of flowers better than yours," Ping said. "It's just this seed that won't grow."

11   Ping's father overheard this and said, "You did your best, and your best is good enough to present to the Emperor."

12   Holding the empty pot in his hands, Ping went straight away to the palace. The Emperor was looking at the flowers slowly, one by one. How beautiful all the flowers were! But the Emperor was frowning and did not say a word.

13   Finally he came to Ping. Ping hung his head in shame, expecting to be punished. The Emperor asked him, "Why did you bring an empty pot?"

14   Ping started to cry and replied, "I planted the seed you gave me and I watered it every day, but it didn't sprout! I tended it all year long, but nothing grew. So today I had to bring an empty pot without a flower. It was the best I could do."

15   When the Emperor heard these words, a smile slowly spread over his face, and he put his arm around Ping. Then he exclaimed to one and all, "I have found him! I have found the one person worthy of being Emperor!

16   "Where you got your seeds from, I don't know. For the seeds I gave you had all been cooked. So it was impossible for any of them to grow.

17   "I admire Ping's great courage to appear before me with the empty truth, and now I reward him with my entire kingdom and make him Emperor of all the land!"

1. **Part A**

   Which choice is the **best** summary of the story?

   ○ A. Ping does not know how to grow plants, so he was unable to grow his plant for the Emperor.

   ○ B. The Emperor wanted to choose a successor, so he decided to let the plants choose. Ping was the only child that was honest about growing his plant, so he became the next Emperor.

   ○ C. Ping took good care of his plant. He watered it every day and gave it rich soil. Even though he took good care of his plant, it would not grow.

   ○ D. The Emperor was old and needed to choose a successor. The Emperor loved flowers, so he decided to let the flowers choose the new Emperor. The Emperor cooked the seeds.

   **Part B**

   Which two sentences from the story **best** support the answer to Part A?

   ☐ A. "Because the Emperor loved flowers so much, he decided to let the flowers choose." (paragraph 3)

   ☐ B. "Spring came, and all the children put on their best clothes to greet the Emperor." (paragraph 8)

   ☐ C. "Ping started to cry and replied, 'I planted the seed you gave me and I watered it every day, but it didn't sprout!'" (paragraph 14)

   ☐ D. "I admire Ping's great courage to appear before me with the empty truth, and now I reward him with my entire kingdom and make him Emperor of all the land!" (paragraph 17)

   ☐ E. "They planted them everywhere, and the air smelled like perfume." (paragraph 2)

   ☐ F. "A long time ago in China there was a boy named Ping who loved flowers." (paragraph 1)

   ☐ G. "Ping was ashamed of his empty pot." (paragraph 9)

**2.** Based on the story, which three character traits **best** describe Ping. Select three traits from the list that best describe Ping by putting a check mark in the boxes next to the three correct answers.

- ☐ A. Foolish
- ☐ B. Lucky
- ☐ C. Honest
- ☐ D. Evil
- ☐ E. Hardworking
- ☐ F. Brave
- ☐ G. Mysterious
- ☐ H. Nice
- ☐ I. Angry

**3. Part A**

What is the theme of this story?

- ○ A. Whoever grows the best flower becomes Emperor.
- ○ B. Honesty is the best policy.
- ○ C. Cooked seeds will never grow.
- ○ D. The best gardeners live in China.

**Part B**

Which sentence from the story **best** supports the answer to Part A?

- ○ A. "I admire Ping's great courage to appear before me with the empty truth, and now I reward him with my entire kingdom and make him Emperor of all the land!" (paragraph 17)
- ○ B. "Children from all over the country swarmed to the palace to get their flower seeds." (paragraph 5)
- ○ C. "A long time ago in China there was a boy named Ping who loved flowers." (paragraph 1)
- ○ D. "When Ping received his seed from the Emperor, he was the happiest child of all." (paragraph 6)

4. **Part A**

Read the sentence from paragraph 4 of "The Empty Pot."

> "The next day a **proclamation** was issued: All the children in the land were to come to the palace."

What does the word **proclamation** mean as it is used in the sentence?

- ○ A. a public announcement
- ○ B. a contest
- ○ C. a warning of danger
- ○ D. a law

**Part B**

Which detail from the story **best** supports the answer to Part A.

- ○ A. "He needed to choose a successor to the throne." (paragraph 2)
- ○ B. "Spring came, and all the children put on their best clothes to greet the Emperor." (paragraph 8)
- ○ C. "This news created great excitement throughout the land!" (paragraph 5)
- ○ D. "Holding the empty pot in his hands, Ping went straight away to the palace." (paragraph 12)

**5.** At the end of the story the Emperor says, "I admire Ping's great courage to appear before me with the empty truth." Write two details from the list below in the boxes that show how Ping demonstrates courage in the story.

| Possible Details |
|---|
| "A long time ago in China there was a boy named Ping who loved flowers." |
| "Ping started to cry and replied, 'I planted the seed you gave me and I watered it every day, but it didn't sprout!'" |
| "When Ping received his seed from the Emperor, he was the happiest child of all." |
| "Ping's father overheard this and said, 'You did your best, and your best is good enough to present to the Emperor.'" |
| "So today I had to bring an empty pot without a flower. It was the best I could do." |
| "'I've grown lots of flowers better than yours,' Ping said. 'It's just this seed that won't grow.'" |

| Details That Show Courage |
|---|
| **Detail #1:** |
| **Detail #2:** |

6. **Prose Constructed Response—Narrative Writing**

In "The Empty Pot," the Emperor needs to find a successor to the throne. Think about the details the author uses to create the characters, settings, and events.

Think about what you know from the story, and write about what will happen next. What will happen when Ping becomes the Emperor of the Kingdom? Use what you have learned about Ping when you are writing your story.

------------------------------------------------

------------------------------------------------

------------------------------------------------

------------------------------------------------

------------------------------------------------

------------------------------------------------

------------------------------------------------

------------------------------------------------

------------------------------------------------

------------------------------------------------

------------------------------------------------

------------------------------------------------

Read "The Secret Language of Dolphins." Then answer the questions.

## The Secret Language of Dolphins
### by Crispin Boyer

1   Here's a conversation worth talking about: A mother dolphin chats with her baby… over the telephone! The special call was made in an aquarium in Hawaii, where the mother and her two-year-old calf swam in separate tanks connected by a special underwater audio link. The two dolphins began squawking and chirping to each other—distinctive dolphin chatter.

## Cracking the Code

2   "It seemed clear that they knew who they were talking with," says Don White, whose Project Delphis ran the experiment. "Information was passing back and forth pretty quickly." But what were they saying? That's what scientists are trying to find out by studying wild and captive dolphins all over the world to decipher their secret language. They haven't completely cracked the code yet, but they're listening . . . and learning.

## Chatty Mammals

3   In many ways, you are just like the more than 30 species of dolphins that swim in the world's oceans and rivers. Dolphins are mammals, like you are, and must swim to the surface to breathe air. Just as you might, they team up in pods, or groups, to accomplish tasks. And they're smart.

4   They also talk to each other. Starting from birth, dolphins squawk, whistle, click, and squeak. "Sometimes one dolphin will vocalize and then another will seem to answer," says Sara Waller, who studies bottlenose dolphins off the California coast. "And sometimes members of a pod vocalize in different patterns at the same time, much like many people chattering at a party." And just as you gesture and change facial expressions as you talk, dolphins

communicate nonverbally through body postures, jaw claps, bubble blowing, and fin caresses.

## Thinking Dolphin

5   Scientists think dolphins "talk" about everything from basic facts like their age to their emotional state. "I speculate that they say things like 'there are some good fish over here,' or 'watch out for that shark because he's hunting,'" says Denise Herzing, who studies dolphins in the Bahamas.

6   When the going gets tough, for instance, some dolphins call for backup. After being bullied by a duo of bottlenose dolphins, one spotted dolphin returned to the scene the next day with a few pals to chase and harass one of the bully bottlenose dolphins. "It's as if the spotted dolphin communicated to his buddies that he needed their help, then led them in search of this guy," says Herzing, who watched the scuffle.

**Language Lessons**

7   Kathleen Dudzinski, director of the Dolphin Communication Project, has listened to dolphins for more than 17 years, using high-tech gear to record and analyze every nuance of their language. But she says she's far from speaking "dolphin" yet. Part of the reason is the elusiveness of the animals. Dolphins are fast swimmers who can stay underwater for up to ten minutes between breaths. "It's like studying an iceberg because they spend most of their lives underwater," Dudzinski says.

8   Deciphering "dolphin speak" is also tricky because their language is so dependent on what they're doing, whether they're playing, fighting, or going after tasty fish. It's no different for humans. Think about when you raise a hand to say hello. Under other circumstances, the same gesture can mean good-bye, stop, or that something costs five bucks. It's the same for dolphins. During fights, for example, dolphins clap their jaws to say "back off!" But they jaw clap while playing, too, as if to show who's king of the underwater playground.

9   "I have not found one particular dolphin behavior that means the same thing every time you see it," says Dudzinski. "If you like mysteries and detective work, then this is the job for you." And who knows—maybe someday you'll get a phone call from a dolphin.

### 7. Part A

What is the main idea of this selection?

- ○ A. Dolphins can talk on the telephone.
- ○ B. Scientists believe that dolphins communicate with each other in a way similar to humans.
- ○ C. There are more than 30 species of dolphins.
- ○ D. High-tech gear can analyze the language of dolphins.

### Part B

What detail from the text **best** supports the main idea that was selected above?

- ○ A. "Here's a conversation worth talking about: A mother dolphin chats with her baby... over the telephone!" (paragraph 1)

- ○ B. "'And sometimes members of a pod vocalize in different patterns at the same time, much like many people chattering at a party.'" (paragraph 4)

- ○ C. "When the going gets tough, for instance, some dolphins call for backup." (paragraph 6)

- ○ D. "In many ways, you are just like the more than 30 species of dolphins that swim in the world's oceans and rivers." (paragraph 3)

### 8. Part A

Read the following sentence from paragraph 3 of "The Secret Language of Dolphins."

> Just as you might, they team up in **pods**, or groups, to accomplish tasks.

What is the meaning of the word **pods** as it is used in the article?

- ○ A. peas
- ○ B. boxes
- ○ C. groups
- ○ D. dolphins

## Part B
What comprehension skill can you use to determine the meaning of the word **pod**?

○ A. context clues
○ B. fact and opinion
○ C. prediction
○ D. drawing conclusions

## 9. Part A
What evidence do scientists have that dolphins' language is dependent on what they are doing?

○ A.   A raised hand means hello, good-bye, and five bucks.
○ B.   They blow bubbles.
○ C.   Dolphins clap their jaws when they are playing and to say "Back off!"
○ D.   They call for backup.

## Part B
What sentence from the text **best** supports your answer to Part A?

○ A.   "I speculate that they say things like 'there are some good fish over here,' or 'watch out for that shark because he's hunting,' says Denise Herzing, who studies dolphins in the Bahamas." (paragraph 5)

○ B.   "'It's as if the spotted dolphin communicated to his buddies that he needed their help, then led them in search of this guy,' says Herzing, who watched the scuffle." (paragraph 6)

○ C.   "Deciphering 'dolphin speak' is also tricky because their language is so dependent on what they're doing, whether they're playing, fighting, or going after tasty fish." (paragraph 8)

○ D.   "Kathleen Dudzinski, director of the Dolphin Communication Project, has listened to dolphins for more than 17 years, using high-tech gear to record and analyze every nuance of their language." (paragraph 7)

**10.** Use the selections below to complete the Venn diagram to show ways that dolphin communication and human communication are alike and different.

- Talks about events and emotions

- Uses clicks and whistles

- Uses words

- Communicates with body language

- Communicates with friends and family

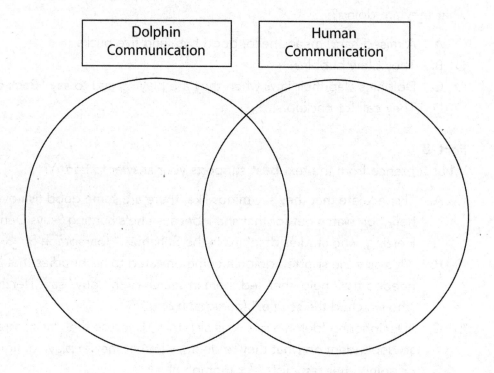

| Dolphin Communication | Human Communication |

**11.** Select two main ideas from the selection below and write them in the boxes labeled Main Idea 1 and Main Idea 2. Then select two supporting details for each main idea from the list below and write them in the boxes underneath each Main Idea.

## Possible Main Ideas

- "In many ways, you are just like the more than 30 species of dolphins that swim in the world's oceans and rivers." (paragraph 3)

- "When the going gets tough, for instance, some dolphins call for backup." (paragraph 6)

- "Scientists think dolphins 'talk' about everything from basic facts like their age to their emotional state." (paragraph 5)

- "Here's a conversation worth talking about: A mother dolphin chats with her baby… over the telephone!" (paragraph 1)

## Possible Supporting Details

- "And just as you gesture and change facial expressions as you talk, dolphins communicate nonverbally through body postures, jaw claps, bubble blowing, and fin caresses." (paragraph 4)

- "The special call was made in an aquarium in Hawaii, where the mother and her two-year-old calf swam in separate tanks connected by a special underwater audio link." (paragraph 1)

- "Just as you might, they team up in pods, or groups, to accomplish tasks." (paragraph 3)

- "After being bullied by a duo of bottlenose dolphins, one spotted dolphin returned to the scene the next day with a few pals to chase and harass one of the bully bottlenose dolphins." (paragraph 6)

- "During fights, for example, dolphins clap their jaws to say 'back off!' But they jaw clap while playing, too, as if to show who's king of the underwater playground." (paragraph 8)

- "'If you like mysteries and detective work, then this is the job for you.'" (paragraph 9)

| Main Idea 1 | Main Idea 2 |
|---|---|
|  |  |

| Supporting Details for Main Idea 1 | Supporting Details for Main Idea 2 |
|---|---|
|  |  |
|  |  |

## Answers

### Unit 1: Literary Analysis Task

#### "Crisis at Crittertown"

1. The correct answer is below.

> **First**
> The mice started to understand human language.

> **Second**
> The mice gave each other names.

> **Third**
> Grayson wanted to go exploring, but Brownback said No.

> **Fourth**
> Brownback agreed to let Grayson go exploring, as long as Cheddar went with him.

> **Fifth**
> The mice got ready to go upstairs and learn about the world.

2. **Part A—(B)** is the correct answer. In this story, colony refers to a group of animals (mice) that live together.

   **Part B—(B)** is the correct answer. This sentence shows that it is a group of animals (mice) that are living together.

3. **Part A—(D)** is the correct answer. Cheddar is careful and does not take risks.

   **Part B—(A)** is the correct answer. Brownback agrees to let the mice go exploring because he knows that Cheddar will keep Grayson safe.

4. **Part A—(D)** is the correct answer. The mice had to move sneakily.

   **Part B—(B)** is the correct answer. The mice had to move sneakily so they would not get caught.

5. The correct answer is below.

| Name | Character Trait |
|------|-----------------|
| Cheddar | Trustworthy |
| Grayson | Daring |
| Brownback | Fair |

6. **Part A—(A)** is the correct answer. When he first arrives at the post office he smells many smells and hears the noise on the radio.

   **Part B—(B)** is the correct answer. It supports the answer to Part A.

7. **Sample Response**

Cheddar is a mouse that likes cheese, a lot! In "Crisis in Crittertown," the mice learn how to understand human language. This made some of the mice want to explore the human world. In this story, Cheddar is cautious and smart.

Cheddar is considered a cautious mouse in the story. This means that he knows how to stay safe, and doesn't take a lot of risks. In the text, Grayson says that Cheddar will keep him in line, and that Cheddar is always holding him back from fun and danger. The leader of the mice, Brownback, says, "Cheddar is cautious and caution keeps a mouse in line!". Cheddar is a voice of reason to Grayson's energy and enthusiasm.

Cheddar is also smart. He is able to read and observe his environment to learn things. In the story he says that he felt "stuffed full of facts". He was also smart to know when to leave the post office so that Brownback would let them come back again. I'm sure he wanted to eat some more cheese crackers!

Cheddar is cautious and smart in the story. He makes sure that Grayson stays safe while they are able to learn, eat, and have an adventure. He took his promise to Brownback seriously. Cheddar is a good mouse to have in the colony.

## "In a Class by Himself"

8. **Part A—(C)** is the correct answer. The other choices reflect less important purposes for writing the story.

   **Part B—(A)** is the correct answer. The author is writing about how Mr. Clark has changed her life because of his actions. This answer choice shows that Mr. Clark helped her to change into a more productive and successful student.

9. **Part A—(A)** is the correct answer.

   **Part B—(D)** is the correct answer. *Snowballs* gives us the best clue to the meaning of the word, because a snowball is something that you throw.

10. **Part A—(D)** is the correct answer.

    **Part B—(C)** is the correct answer. This sentence from the text explains how Mr. Clark has helped to change her life.

11. The answer to the question is below. Compassionate and ambitious are the two best character traits that describe Mr. Clark. Compassionate means caring, and ambitious means hardworking. Both of these traits describe Mr. Clark. The evidence listed below supports these traits.

| Column 1<br>Character Trait | Column 2<br>Evidence |
|---|---|
| Compassionate | I was wrong. That first week, I kept mocking him. He hauled me out to the hallway and said I'd better shape up. "Tamara," he said, "you're a smart kid. You can do better." |
| Ambitious | He came to Harlem because he'd seen a TV show about our troubled schools and the lack of qualified teachers. He wanted a challenge. Boy, did he get one. |

12. The answer to the question is below.

| Event | Supporting Detail |
|---|---|
| Tamara is acting up in class. | He told me I was a natural leader and that I'd go far in life if I started applying myself. |
| The students needed to improve their grades. | Mr. Clark worked long hours, making sure I did my work. |
| Mr. Clark wins the Disney Teacher of the Year Award. | But when it came time to draw names, Mr. Clark said, "You're all going." |

## Unit 2: Research Simulation Task

1. **Part A—(C)** is the correct answer. In this sentence, conserve means to save energy.

   **Part B—(C)** is the correct answer. It shows how to save energy by staying still.

2. **Part A—(C)** is the correct answer. It is important to plan so that you can pack needed items that would help you in case of an emergency.

   **Part B—(A)** is the correct answer. This answer choice shows some of the items that would be helpful to pack before your trip.

3. **Part A—(D)** is the correct answer. The article is mostly about how to pack and use items to maintain your safety in the wilderness.

   **Part B—(C) and (E)** are the correct answers. These sentences show how preparation is important and can help in an emergency.

4. **Part A—(D)** is the correct answer. In this article, expedition means a trip into the wilderness.

   **Part B—(C)** is the correct answer. You take a trip into a territory.

5. **Part A—(B)** is the correct answer. This article is written to inform readers about how to stay safe in the wilderness.

   **Part B—(B)** is the correct answer. This answer provides a fact about how to stay safe in the wilderness.

6. **(A), (C), and (F)** are the correct answers. All three of these are stated in both articles. The other statements are only reflected in one of the articles.

7. The answer to the question is below.

| True | False |
|------|-------|
| Water found in nature should be boiled before it is consumed. | You should not be concerned with animals in the wild. |
| Bad weather requires you to find shelter quickly. | You should walk around and try and find your way out if you become lost. |
| You will need to find water more quickly than food. | |

8. **Sample Response**

## Preparation Is the Key to Safety— How to Survive in the Wilderness

Getting lost in the wilderness is serious and can be life threatening. With some knowledge and preparation, you can stay safe until help arrives.

Before you go on a hike, you need to prepare. Tell someone where you are going and what time you are expected to return. This is important so that someone knows to look for you if you don't return on time. Be sure to pack useful supplies such as matches, garbage bags, a flashlight, and a whistle. These can be used for a variety of tasks such as signaling, boiling water, and making shelter. Pack water and snacks that have protein and carbohydrates in them. Water is the most important thing that your body will need, but snacks will help too!

While you are in the wilderness, if you become lost, the first thing to do is stop. This allows you to conserve your energy and come up with a plan. When you are thinking about your plan consider shelter, water, and signaling. Shelter will protect you from the weather and animals. Water is critical, and must be found or collected and boiled. While you are waiting for help to arrive, be aware of any animals that might be around you. Some of them can be dangerous, but most animals will not bother you unless you bother them.

You also need to figure out ways to attract attention. This can be done with a whistle, a fire, or even by waving your arms or a brightly colored bandana. Be sure to try and attract attention so that someone can find you. If you stay calm, create a plan, and meet your basic needs, this will increase your chances of being rescued.

# Unit 3: Narrative Writing Task

1. **Part A—(B)** is the correct answer. The other choices do not give a complete summary of the entire story.

   **Part B—(C) and (D)** are the correct answers. They support the summary selected in Part A.

2. **(C), (E), and (F)** are the correct answers to this question. Ping is honest because he brings the plant that "grew" from the seed that the Emperor gave him. He is hardworking because he takes care of his plant by watering it daily, changing the soil, etc. He is brave because he faced the Emperor even though he is ashamed of his flower.

3. **Part A—(B)** is the correct answer. Honesty is the best policy. In the story, Ping is honest, and because of that he gets to be the next Emperor.

   **Part B—(A)** is the correct answer. It supports the theme selected in Part A.

4. **Part A—(A)** is the correct answer. A proclamation is a public announcement. The proclamation was made to announce that the Emperor needed a successor.

   **Part B—(C)** is the correct answer. It supports the definition selected in Part A.

5. **Detail 1**—Ping started to cry and replied, "I planted the seed you gave me and I watered it every day, but it didn't sprout!

   **Detail 2**—So today I had to bring an empty pot without a flower. It was the best I could do."

   Both of these details show ways that Ping had courage when facing the Emperor. He was scared, but he told the truth.

6. **Sample Response**

On a bright and sunny day, Ping became the leader of the Kingdom. The young Emperor Ping was nervous about his new role as the leader of the Kingdom. When Emperor Ping told his father about his worries, his father reminded him that he was brave and a hard worker. He could use these skills to solve any problem that might come his way. Ping knew that his father was right. Ping felt better, and he began to focus on the job of running the Kingdom.

Ping's first few weeks as the Emperor were uneventful. His family moved into the palace, and Ping began to learn about how running the Kingdom worked. Every morning he would wake up and water the beautiful flowers that surrounded the palace. This gave him a chance to think about the people in his Kingdom and what they might need.

One morning while he was watering the plants, a man visited Ping. The man was tall and wore long dark robes. The man told Ping that he was an oracle, and that he could see into the future. He told Emperor Ping that he had a vision of a strong rainstorm that would last for weeks that would flood the Kingdom. He told Ping that he needed to move the people in the Kingdom to higher ground so that they would be safe from the storm. He urged Ping to act quickly, because there wasn't much time before the storm would come.

Ping was worried. How would he get all of the people to move to higher ground? He decided to make a proclamation to the Kingdom about the storm that was coming and to order the people to move to a safer place. Ping issued his proclamation, and the people of the Kingdom laughed.

"Look, the sun is shining!" said a man.

A woman said, "You are just a child, why should we listen to you?"

Ping was discouraged. He knew he needed a plan to save everyone, but they wouldn't listen to him. Ping went to water his flowers and think about how he might solve this problem. As he was staring at his flowers, he had an idea. He had a beautiful garden, and the palace was the highest point in the Kingdom. If he could get everyone to come to the palace on the day of the storm, they would be safe and see that they could trust him.

The next morning, Ping woke up and he saw that the sky was gray. He knew that today was the day that the storm would come. Ping worked quickly. He sent all of his servants out to invite the people to come see his garden and have a delicious lunch at the palace at noon. Ping asked the chefs to prepare their most delicious foods so that the smells would drift all through the Kingdom.

As the people smelled the food, and heard the invitation, they were excited. They forgot all about Ping's warning and headed to the palace to see the beautiful flowers and eat the lunch. By noon the entire Kingdom was at the palace eating and talking and looking at the flowers. Suddenly, there was a huge clap of thunder and rain started pouring from the sky.

Everyone looked at the Emperor and realized that his prediction was true. They were happy that their friends and family were safe from the flood. From that point on, the people of the town trusted Ping because they knew he was brave and smart. He had worked hard to keep them safe, even when they didn't believe him. They knew he was the right Emperor for their Kingdom.

## "The Secret Language of Dolphins"

7. **Part A—(B)** is the correct answer. Dolphins and humans communicate in many similar ways.

   **Part B—(D)** is the correct answer. This sentence shows that humans and dolphins communicate in similar ways.

8. **Part A—(C)** is the correct answer. A pod is a group of dolphins.

   **Part B—(A)** is the correct strategy. Context clues can be used to determine the answer. A context clue is a clue within the sentence or sentences around the unknown word.

9. **Part A—(C)** is the correct answer. This answer shows an example of how a jaw clap can mean that they are playing or issuing a threat.

   **Part B—(C)** is the correct answer. This answer shows how dolphin language can change based on the situation.

10. The correct answer is below.

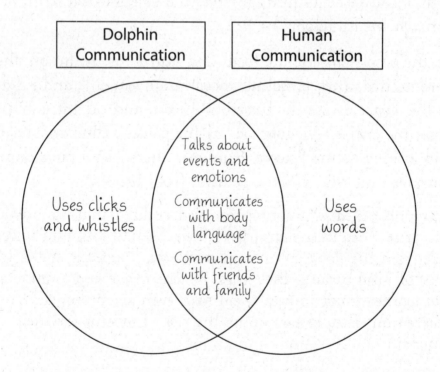

11. The correct answer is below.

| Main Idea 1 | Main Idea 2 |
|---|---|
| In many ways, you are just like the more than 30 species of dolphins that swim in the world's oceans and rivers. | Scientists think dolphins "talk" about everything from basic facts like their age to their emotional state. |
| **Supporting Details for Main Idea 1** | **Supporting Details for Main Idea 2** |
| Just as you might, they team up in pods, or groups, to accomplish tasks. | During fights, for example, dolphins clap their jaws to say "back off!" But they jaw clap while playing, too, as if to show who's king of the underwater playground. |
| And just as you gesture and change facial expressions as you talk, dolphins communicate nonverbally through body postures, jaw claps, bubble blowing, and fin caresses. | After being bullied by a duo of bottlenose dolphins, one spotted dolphin returned to the scene the next day with a few pals to chase and harass one of the bully bottlenose dolphins. |

# Writing Rubrics

## Narrative Writing Rubric (July 2015)

| | Construct Measured |
|---|---|
| | Written Expression |
| **Score Point 3** | The student response:<br><br>—is effectively developed with narrative elements and is consistently appropriate to the task.<br>—is effectively organized with clear and coherent writing.<br>—uses language effectively to clarify ideas. |
| **Score Point 2** | The student response:<br><br>—is developed with some narrative elements and is generally appropriate to the task.<br>—is organized with mostly coherent writing.<br>—uses language that is mostly effective to clarify ideas. |
| **Score Point 1** | The student response:<br><br>—is minimally developed with few narrative elements and is limited in its appropriateness to the task.<br>—demonstrates limited organization and coherence.<br>—uses language to express ideas with limited clarity. |
| **Score Point 0** | The student response:<br><br>—is undeveloped and/or inappropriate to the task.<br>—lacks organization and coherence.<br>—does not use language to express ideas with clarity. |

| Construct Measured | |
| --- | --- |
| Knowledge of Language and Conventions | |
| Score Point 3 | The student response to the prompt demonstrates full command of the conventions of standard English at an appropriate level of complexity. There may be a few minor errors in mechanics, grammar, and usage, but meaning is clear. |
| Score Point 2 | The student response to the prompt demonstrates some command of the conventions of standard English at an appropriate level of complexity. There may be errors in mechanics, grammar, and usage that occasionally impede understanding, but the meaning is generally clear |
| Score Point 1 | The student response to the prompt demonstrates limited command of the conventions of standard English at an appropriate level of complexity. There may be errors in mechanics, grammar, and usage that often impede understanding. |
| Score Point 0 | The student response to the prompt does not demonstrate command of the conventions of standard English at the appropriate level of complexity. There are frequent and varied errors in mechanics, grammar, and usage that impede understanding. |

# Literary Analysis and Research Writing Rubric (July 2015)

| | Reading Comprehension and Written Expression<br>The student response: |
|---|---|
| Score Point 4 | —demonstrates full comprehension of ideas stated explicitly and/or inferentially by providing an accurate analysis.<br>—addresses the prompt and provides effective development of the topic that is consistently appropriate to task, purpose, and audience.<br>—uses clear reasoning supported by relevant, text-based evidence in the development of the topic.<br>—is effectively organized with clear and coherent writing.<br>—uses language effectively to clarify ideas. |
| Score Point 3 | —demonstrates comprehension of ideas stated explicitly and/or inferentially by providing a mostly accurate analysis.<br>—addresses the prompt and provides mostly effective development of the topic that is appropriate to task, purpose, and audience.<br>—uses mostly clear reasoning supported by relevant text-based evidence in the development of the topic.<br>—is organized with mostly clear and coherent writing.<br>—uses language that is mostly effective to clarify ideas. |
| Score Point 2 | —demonstrates basic comprehension of ideas stated explicitly and/or inferentially by providing a generally accurate analysis.<br>—addresses the prompt and provides some development of the topic that is somewhat appropriate to task, purpose, and audience.<br>—uses some reasoning and text-based evidence in the development of the topic.<br>—demonstrates some organization with somewhat coherent writing.<br>—uses language to express ideas with some clarity. |

| Score Point 1 | —demonstrates limited comprehension of ideas by providing a minimally accurate analysis.<br>—addresses the prompt and provides minimal development of the topic that is limited in its appropriateness to task, purpose, and audience.<br>—uses limited reasoning and text-based evidence.<br>—demonstrates limited organization and coherence.<br>—uses language to express ideas with limited clarity. |
|---|---|
| Score Point 0 | —demonstrates no comprehension of ideas by providing an inaccurate or no analysis.<br>—is undeveloped and/or inappropriate to the task, purpose, and audience.<br>—includes little to no text-based evidence.<br>—lacks organization and coherence.<br>—does not use language to express ideas with clarity. |

| Knowledge of Language and Conventions || 
|---|---|
| **The student response:** ||
| Score Point 3 | —The student response to the prompt demonstrates full command of the conventions of standard English at an appropriate level of complexity. There may be a few minor errors in mechanics, grammar, and usage, but meaning is clear. |
| Score Point 2 | —The student response to the prompt demonstrates some command of the conventions of standard English at an appropriate level of complexity. There may be errors in mechanics, grammar, and usage that occasionally impede understanding, but the meaning is generally clear. |
| Score Point 1 | —The student response to the prompt demonstrates limited command of the conventions of standard English at an appropriate level of complexity. There may be errors in mechanics, grammar, and usage that often impede understanding. |
| Score Point 0 | —The student response to the prompt does not demonstrate command of the conventions of standard English at the appropriate level of complexity. Frequent and varied errors in mechanics, grammar, and usage impede understanding. |

# Common Core Standards—Grade 4

| RL: Reading Standards for Literature |
| --- |
| **Key Ideas and Details** |
| **RL.4.1:** Refer to details and examples in a text when explaining what the text says explicitly and when drawing inferences from the text. |
| **RL.4.2:** Determine a theme of a story, drama, or poem from details in the text; summarize the text. |
| **RL.4.3:** Describe in depth a character, setting, or event in a story or drama, drawing on specific details in the text (e.g., a character's thoughts, words, or actions). |
| **Craft and Structure** |
| **RL.4.4:** Determine the meaning of words and phrases as they are used in a text, including those that allude to significant characters found in mythology (e.g., *Herculean*), drawing on a wide reading of classic myths from a variety of cultures and periods. |
| **RL.4.5:** Explain major differences between poems, drama, and prose, and refer to the core structural elements of poems (e.g., stanza, verse, rhythm, meter) and drama (e.g., casts of characters, setting descriptions, dialogue, acts, scenes, stage directions) when writing or speaking about a text. |
| **RL.4.6:** Compare and contrast the point of view from which different stories are narrated, including the difference between first- and third-person narrations. |
| **Integration of Knowledge and Ideas** |
| **RL.4.7:** Integrate information gained from illustrations and other visual elements in a text with the words to demonstrate understanding of how the characters, setting, and plot interact and develop. |
| **RL.4.8:** (Not applicable to literature) |

| RL: Reading Standards for Literature |
|---|
| **RL.4.9:** Compare and contrast the treatment of similar themes and topics (e.g., opposition of good and evil) and patterns of events (e.g., the quest) in stories, myths, and traditional literature from different cultures. |
| **Range of Reading and Level of Text Complexity** |
| **RL.4.10:** By the end of the year, read and comprehend literature, including stories, dramas, and poetry, in the grades 4–5 text complexity band proficiently, with scaffolding as needed at the high end of the range. |

| RL: Reading Standards for Informational Text |
|---|
| **A: Key Ideas and Details** |
| **RI.4.1:** Refer to details and examples in a text when explaining what the text says explicitly and when drawing inferences from the text. |
| **RI.4.2:** Determine the main idea of a text and explain how it is supported by key details; summarize the text. |
| **RI.4.3:** Explain events, procedures, ideas, or concepts in a historical, scientific, or technical text, including what happened and why, based on specific information in the text. |
| **Craft and Structure** |
| **RI.4.4:** Determine the meaning of general academic and domain-specific words or phrases in a text relevant to a *grade 4 topic or subject area*. |
| **RI.4.5:** Describe the overall structure of events, ideas, concepts, or information (e.g., chronology, comparison, cause/effect) in a text or part of a text. |
| **RI.4.6:** Compare and contrast a firsthand and secondhand account of the same event or topic; describe the differences in focus and the information provided. |

| RL: Reading Standards for Informational Text |
|---|

### Integration of Knowledge and Ideas

**RI.4.7:** Interpret factual information presented graphically or visually (e.g., in charts, graphs, diagrams, time lines, animations, or interactive elements on Web pages) and explain how the information contributes to understanding the text in which they appear.

**RI.4.8:** Explain how an author uses reasons and evidence to support particular points in a text.

**RI.4.9:** Integrate information from two texts on the same topic in order to write or speak about the subject knowledgeably.

### Range of Reading and Level of Text Complexity

**RI.4.10:** By the end of year, read and comprehend informational texts, including historical, scientific, and technical texts, in the grades 4–5 text complexity band proficiently, with scaffolding as necessary at the high end of the range.

| RF: Foundational Skills |
|---|

### Phonics and Word Recognition

**RF.4.1:** Know and apply grade-level phonics and word analysis skills in decoding words.

  a. Use combined knowledge of all letter-sound correspondences, syllabication patterns, and morphology (e.g., roots and affixes) to read accurately unfamiliar multi-syllabic words in context and out of context.

### Fluency

**RF.4.2:** Read with sufficient accuracy and fluency to support comprehension.

  a. Read on-level text with purpose and understanding.
  b. Read on-level prose and poetry orally with accuracy, appropriate rate, and expression.
  c. Use context to confirm or self-correct word recognition and understanding, rereading as necessary.

## SL: Speaking and Listening

### A: Comprehension and Collaboration

**SL.4.1**: Engage effectively in range of collaborative discussions (one-on-one and in groups) on *grade 4 topics and texts*, building on others' ideas and expressing their own clearly.

  a. Come to discussions prepared, having read or studied required material; explicitly draw on that preparation and other information known about the topic to explore ideas under discussions.
  b. Follow agreed-upon rules for discussions and carry out assigned roles.
  c. Pose and respond to specific questions to clarify or follow up on information, and make comments that contribute to the discussion and link to the remarks of others.
  d. Review the key ideas expressed and explain their own ideas and understanding in light of the discussion.

**SL.4.2**: Paraphrase portions of written texts read aloud or information presented graphically, orally, visually, or multimodally.

**SL.4.3**: Identify the reasons and evidence a speaker provides to support particular points.

### B: Presentation of Knowledge and Ideas

**SL.4.4**: Report on a topic or text, tell a story, or recount an experience in an organized manner, using appropriate facts and relevant, descriptive details to support main ideas or themes; speak clearly at an understandable pace.

**SL.4.5**: Add audio recordings and visual displays to presentations when appropriate to enhance the development of main ideas or themes.

**SL.4.6**: Differentiate between contexts that call for formal English (e.g., presenting ideas) and situations where informal discourse is appropriate (e.g., small-group discussion); use formal English when appropriate to task and situation.

## W: Writing Standards

### Text Types and Purposes

**W.4.1:** Write opinion pieces on topics or texts, supporting a point of view with reasons and information.

   a.  Introduce a topic or text clearly, state an opinion, and create an organizational structure in which related ideas are grouped to support the writer's purpose.

   b.  Provide reasons that are supported by facts and details.

   c.  Link opinion and reasons using words and phrases (e.g., *for instance, in order to, in addition*).

   d.  Provide a concluding statement or section related to the opinion presented

**W.4.2:** Write informative/explanatory texts to examine a topic and convey ideas and information clearly.

   a.  Introduce a topic clearly and group related information in paragraphs and sections; include formatting (e.g., headings), illustrations, and multimedia when useful to aiding comprehension.

   b.  Develop the topic with facts, definitions, concrete details, quotations, or other information and examples related to the topic.

   c.  Link ideas within categories of information using words and phrases (e.g., *another, for example, also, because*).

   d.  Use precise language and domain-specific vocabulary to inform about or explain the topic.

   e.  Provide a concluding statement or section related to the information or explanation presented.

## W: Writing Standards

**W.4.3:** Write narratives to develop real or imagined experiences or events using effective technique, descriptive details, and clear event sequences.

    a. Orient the reader by establishing a situation and introducing a narrator and/or characters; organize an event sequence that unfolds naturally.

    b. Use dialogue and description to develop experiences and events or show the responses of characters to situations.

    c. Use a variety of transitional words and phrases to manage the sequence of events.

    d. Use concrete words and phrases and sensory details to convey experiences and events precisely.

    e. Provide a conclusion that follows from the narrated experiences or events.

### Production and Distribution of Writing

**W.4.4:** Produce clear and coherent writing in which the development and organization are appropriate to task, purpose, and audience. (Grade-specific expectations for writing types are defined in standards 1–3 above.)

**W.4.5:** With guidance and support from peers and adults, develop and strengthen writing as needed by planning, revising, and editing.

**W.4.6:** With some guidance and support from adults, use technology, including the Internet, to produce and publish writing (using the keyboard) as well as to interact and collaborate with others.

### Research to Build Knowledge

**W.4.7:** Conduct short research projects that build knowledge through investigation of different aspects of a topic.

**W.4.8:** Recall relevant information from experiences or gather relevant information from print and digital sources; take notes and categorize information, and provide a list of sources.

## W: Writing Standards

**W.4.9:** Draw evidence from literary or informational texts to support analysis, reflection, and research.

a. Apply *grade 4 Reading standards* to literature (e.g., describe in depth a character, setting, or event in a story or drama, drawing on specific details in the text).

b. Apply *grade 4 Reading standards* to informational texts (e.g., explain how an author uses reasons and evidence to support particular points in a text).

### Range of Writing

**W.4.10:** Write routinely over extended time frames (time for research, reflection, and revision) and shorter time frames (a single sitting or a day or two) for a range of discipline-specific tasks, purposes, and audiences.

## L: Language Standards

### Conventions

**L.4.1:** Observe conventions of grammar and usage when writing or speaking.

a. Use relative pronouns (*who, whose, whom, which, that*) and relative adverbs (*where, when, why*).

b. Form and use the progressive (e.g., *I was walking; I am walking; I will be walking*) verb aspects.

c. Use modal auxiliaries (e.g., *can, may, must*) to convey various conditions.

d. Order adjectives within sentences according to conventional patterns (e.g., *a small red bag* rather than *a red small bag*).

e. Form and use prepositional phrases.

f. Produce complete sentences, recognizing and correcting rhetorically poor fragments and run-ons.

g. Correctly use frequently confused words (e.g., *to, too, two; there, their*).

## L: Language Standards

**L.4.2:** Observe conventions of capitalization, punctuation, and spelling when writing.

    a.  Use correct capitalization.

    b.  Use commas and quotation marks to mark direct speech and quotations from a text.

    c.  Use a comma before a coordinating conjunction in a compound sentence.

    d.  Spell grade-appropriate words correctly, consulting references as needed.

### Effective Language Use

**L.4.3:** Use language to enhance meaning and achieve particular effects when writing or speaking.

    a.  Choose words and phrases to convey ideas precisely.

    b.  Use punctuation for effect.

### Vocabulary Acquisition and Usage

**L.4.4:** Determine or clarify the meaning of unknown and multiple-meaning words and phrases based on *grade 4 reading and content*, choosing flexibly from a range of strategies.

    a.  Use context (e.g., definitions, examples, or restatements in text) as a clue to the meaning of a word or phrase.

    b.  Use common, grade-appropriate Greek and Latin affixes and roots as clues to the meaning of a word (e.g., *telegraph, photograph, autograph*).

    c.  Consult reference materials (e.g., dictionaries, glossaries, thesauruses), both print and digital, to find the pronunciation and determine or clarify the precise meaning of key words and phrases.

## L: Language Standards

**L.4.5:** Demonstrate understanding of figurative language, word relationships, and nuances in word meanings.

   a. Explain the meaning of simple similes and metaphors (e.g., *as pretty as a picture*) in context.
   b. Recognize and explain the meaning of common idioms, adages, and proverbs.
   c. Demonstrate understanding of words by relating them to their opposites (antonyms) and to words with similar but not identical meanings (synonyms).

**L.4.6:** Acquire and use accurately grade-appropriate general academic and domain-specific vocabulary, including words and phrases that signal precise actions, emotions, or states of being (e.g., *quizzed, whined, stammered*) and words and phrases basic to a particular topic (e.g., *wildlife, conservation,* and *endangered* when discussing animal preservation).

# Index

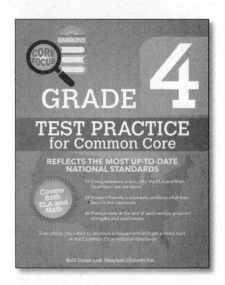